The Drive to Learn

RELATED PUBLICATIONS BY CORNELIUS N. GROVE

Communication across Cultures: A Report on Cross-Cultural Research. National Education Association, 1976.

Cross-Cultural and Other Problems Affecting the Education of Immigrant Portuguese Students in a Program of Transitional Bilingual Education: A Descriptive Case Study. Ed.D. dissertation, Columbia University, 1977.

U.S. Schooling through Chinese Eyes. *Phi Delta Kappan*, 65(7), 1984.

Secondary Education in the United States: An Overview for Educators from Abroad. Council on International Educational Exchange, 1990.

How People from Different Cultures Expect *to Learn*. GROVEWELL LLC, 2003.

Understanding the Two Instructional Style Prototypes: Pathways to Success in Internationally Diverse Classrooms. In *International Communication Competencies in Higher Education and Management.* 2006.

Encountering the Chinese: A Modern Country, an Ancient Culture (3rd ed., 2010; 1st ed., 1999). With coauthors Hu Wenzhong and Zhuang Enping.

The Aptitude Myth: How an Ancient Belief Came to Undermine Children's Learning Today. 2013.

Culturally Responsive Pedagogy. In *Encyclopedia of Intercultural Competence.* 2015.

Pedagogy across Cultures. In *International Encyclopedia of Intercultural Communication.* 2018.

The Drive to Learn

What the East Asian Experience Tells Us about Raising Students Who Excel

Cornelius N. Grove

ROWMAN & LITTLEFIELD
Lanham • Boulder • New York • London

Published by Rowman & Littlefield
A wholly owned subsidiary of The Rowman & Littlefield Publishing Group, Inc.
4501 Forbes Boulevard, Suite 200, Lanham, Maryland 20706
www.rowman.com

Unit A, Whitacre Mews, 26-34 Stannary Street, London SE11 4AB

Copyright © 2017 by Cornelius N. Grove

All rights reserved. No part of this book may be reproduced in any form or by any electronic or mechanical means, including information storage and retrieval systems, without written permission from the publisher, except by a reviewer who may quote passages in a review.

British Library Cataloguing in Publication Information Available

Library of Congress Cataloging-in-Publication Data Available

ISBN: 978-1-4758-1509-2 (cloth: alk. paper)
ISBN: 978-1-4758-1510-8 (paper)
ISBN: 978-1-4758-1511-5 (electronic)

∞™ The paper used in this publication meets the minimum requirements of American National Standard for Information Sciences—Permanence of Paper for Printed Library Materials, ANSI/NISO Z39.48-1992.

Printed in the United States of America

[In America,] you didn't really have to really, really do it.

—"Seiji," a sixth-grade student in Japan who returned the previous year from five years of schooling in the United States. He was commenting on the difference in academic expectations in Japan and the United States.

Contents

Preface ... xi
    Why I Wrote *The Drive to Learn* ... xi
    Receptive to Learning ... xii
    How I Came to Write This Book ... xiii

Acknowledgments ... xvii

Introduction ... xix
    An Overview of How This Book Proceeds ... xx
    The Plan of This Book ... xxi
    About This Book ... xxiv

1 Discovery Step 1: Daring to Seek Answers ... 1
    The Question, Restated ... 3
    The Parts of the Paradox ... 4
    Reviewing Step 1 of the Discovery Process ... 6
    Further Reading ... 6

2 Discovery Step 2: Evaluating Eyewitness Reports ... 7
    Questioning the Eyewitness Reports ... 7
    Passiveness in Class ... 8
    Rote Memorizing ... 11
    How Step 2 Advanced Our Discovery Process ... 14
    Further Reading ... 15

3 Discovery Step 3: Exploring Motivations ... 17
    The Agony of Defeat ... 18
    Why Motivations Differ ... 20

	How Step 3 Advanced Our Discovery Process	23
	Further Reading	24
4	Discovery Step 4: Analyzing Determination	25
	From China to America	25
	Deep Meanings of *Learning*	27
	How Step 4 Advanced Our Discovery Process	32
	Further Reading	33
5	Discovery Step 5: Assessing Emotional Drive	35
	Self and Family	36
	Mothers and Motivation	38
	Self, Emotion, and the Drive to Learn	43
	How Step 5 Advanced Our Discovery Process	44
	Further Reading	45
6	Discovery Step 6: Thinking like a Sociologist	47
	Learning in Different Societies	48
	Learning to Be Competent; Learning in School	52
	The Episode with the Key	54
	How Step 6 Advanced Our Discovery Process	55
	Further Reading	56
7	Discovery Step 7: Thinking like a Historian	59
	Taming Students in America	60
	Taming Students in East Asia	62
	Explaining East Asians' Drive to Learn	64
	How Step 7 Advanced Our Discovery Process	66
	Further Reading	67
8	Discovery Step 8: Revealing How Parents Think	69
	The Outward Focus of the East Asian Family	70
	Two Approaches to Raising Children	71
	How the Chinese Talk about Parenting	73
	How the Japanese Talk about Parenting	74
	Cheerleaders and Coaches	76
	How Step 8 Advanced Our Discovery Process	77
	Further Reading	78
9	Discovery Step 9: Revealing What Parents Do	81
	Maintain Very High Expectations . . . Consistently	82
	Intervene to Ensure That High Expectations Are Met	84
	A Revealing Study of Mothers and Children	87
	How Step 9 Advanced Our Discovery Process	90
	Further Reading	90

10	So What Should We Do?	93
	What Are Our Options?	94
	So What Should *Families* Do?	97
	Parenting with *Gŭan*: Seven Commitments to Your Child	98
	Further Reading	100
11	Responsibility and Creativity	103
	Responsibility	103
	Creativity	108
	Further Reading	111

Postscript	113
Notes	117
Bibliography [Non-annotated]	141
A Note about the Online Annotated Bibliography	151
The Story behind this Book's Cover Photo	154

Preface

Did you ever notice that ideas for improving American education are almost entirely about what our *educators* should be doing differently to increase our children's learning?

Children's learning in school is an outcome of daily interactions among them and the adults who work there. But whenever we try to figure out why our children are learning so little, we look only at the *adults*—at factors controlled by adults such as teachers and policy makers.

Get ready for something completely different. I'm going to look only at the *children.*

WHY I WROTE *THE DRIVE TO LEARN*

Across decades, virtually every measure of American children's learning in school has come up with depressing findings. Countless books and articles have offered remedies for why our children fall short. They've all proposed changes in adult-controlled policies and practices: teacher training, textbooks, curricula, high-stakes tests, class size, homework, public or private control. . . .

I believe that our children's poor learning cannot be *totally* the fault of American educators. Our children are active participants in what goes on in schools. If there's a problem with how well our children are learning, *then our children are a part of that problem*.

In this book, I'm going to explain what our children's part is, and what can be done about it.

The Benefits of Looking at the Children

We'll benefit in three ways from looking at the children's part of our educational problem:

- By examining the role of our children, we'll come closer to attaining *a thorough explanation for learning outcomes* that almost all Americans judge to be embarrassingly poor.
- By focusing attention on our children's contribution to the learning process, we will *reduce the burden of blame on educators and policy makers* for poor learning outcomes.
- By considering those who do the learning instead of those who deliver the lessons, we'll see *fresh possibilities for turning around the educational trajectory of our children*.

The People for Whom This Book Was Written

I've written *The Drive to Learn* for Americans who play a role of any kind in children's growth, development, and learning during the first decade of their lives:

- parents and other caretakers of young children, and those who will become parents;
- those who influence parents: authors, advisers, journalists, and parenting advocates;
- teachers and other educators who work with children in pre-kindergarten through upper elementary;
- those who influence early childhood educators such as thought leaders and teacher trainers; and
- citizens who share my deep concern about the faltering outcomes of American schools.

RECEPTIVE TO LEARNING

My raw material for preparing this book was hundreds of research reports by anthropologists and other social scientists who studied children's learning and child-raising in East Asia. Why East Asia? Because there had long been evidence that children there were learning more in schools than children were learning in American schools. Many of the researchers also compared what they were discovering in East Asia with findings from similar research here in the United States.

The more deeply I familiarized myself with this research, the more I became convinced of this:

When compared with East Asian children, American children are *less receptive* to school learning.

"Receptive" is a word you don't often hear. A more common word would be "attentive," "focused," or "interested." Let's use "receptive" because we need an uncommon word to signal an uncommon state of mind. In this book, "receptive to school learning" will mean that a child . . .

- feels deeply committed to learning in school—is *ready*;
- expects to work persistently in order to learn well—is *willing*; and
- knows *how to participate* in the process of learning in school—is *able*.

Being "receptive to learning" is not about whether children have finished their homework, slept at least seven hours, enjoyed a nutritious breakfast, or had enough playground time to blow off excess energy. Those are all important. But here we're thinking about something else.

It comes down to this. We Americans talk a lot about remedies for poor learning in schools. The ones who are learning poorly are the children. Children are part of the problem, so they must be part of the solution. To help us think about the children, we have hundreds of research studies (a) from East Asia, where children learn well, and (b) from the United States, where they don't.

Those studies show that, when compared with East Asian children, American children are *less receptive* to school learning. In this book, you'll discover how I reached that conclusion and how Americans can benefit from knowing *why East Asian children are more receptive in school.*

HOW I CAME TO WRITE THIS BOOK

After gaining a B.A. and a Master of Arts in Teaching degree, I taught high school for four years and worked in educational publishing for a few more. Then my English wife and I quit our jobs and took the liner *France* to Europe. We traveled around Europe and Africa for a year, and lived in rural Portugal for another year. What impelled me to leave the United States for two years?

Let's call it curiosity about other people's values and ways of life. Upon returning I entered Teachers College, Columbia University, preparing to be a high school guidance counselor. One day I found myself eating lunch with a professor who knew a great deal about other people's values and ways of life. Inside me, something clicked. The next day I changed my major.

Two years later, I was doing my doctoral dissertation research in a Massachusetts town to which many Portuguese had immigrated. Over three months, I observed the immigrant students in classes and interviewed them, their parents, and their teachers. My understanding of the impact of cultural values on classroom learning outcomes was broadened and deepened.[1]

As a lecturer at Teachers College and New School University, I taught a graduate course on culture in the classroom. Not wanting a full-time professorial career, I joined the staff of AFS, the student exchange organization. And I finagled an invitation to teach at a Beijing university, after which I joined a Chinese professor to write a book on how to adapt to Chinese culture.[2]

In 1990, I founded the global business leadership consultancy GROVEWELL LLC. A few years later, GROVEWELL was hired to improve the effectiveness of corporate trainers facing learners from multiple nations. This assignment reignited my desire to understand the impact of culture on classroom learning outcomes. So I dived back into the research literature. One result was that I was able to deliver a conference paper in Singapore on how teachers could increase their effectiveness with students from different cultures.[3]

My Recent Path to Writing This Book

In 2007, I began writing a book, one that would enable Americans to appreciate the impact of cultural values on children's activities and outcomes related to classroom learning.

My research for the Singapore paper had reminded me that most Americans assume that how well a child performs in school is largely determined by his or her inborn aptitude. In much of the rest of the world, people assume that a child's *effort* (or the lack of it) is what matters. How did we Americans come to hold this unusual assumption? I began by drafting a chapter to answer that question. It got longer . . . and longer . . . and became *The Aptitude Myth*, published in 2013.

I began a second time to write a book that would enable Americans to appreciate the impact of cultural values on classroom learning. My work on *The Aptitude Myth* had reminded me of the cultural values of the students themselves—values learned from their parents. What assumptions were parents from different cultures making about their children's capacity for, and process of, learning new skills? *Those assumptions affect how well their children will learn in classrooms.*

Around this time, I was invited to contribute entries to a new encyclopedia, the *Encyclopedia of Intercultural Competence*. One of those entries was "Culturally Appropriate Pedagogy." When I'd finished that, I was invited to contribute longer entries to another, more scholarly, encyclopedia, the *Inter-*

national Encyclopedia of Intercultural Communication; one was "Pedagogy across Cultures." To write these, I had to further explore the anthropological research literature.[4]

My Raw Material for Writing This Book

So when I began writing again, I was more aware than ever of the trove of research into school learning. There were mounds of research into parenting, family life, and child development, too. It all revealed the powerful and pervasive influence on each child of the assumptions, expectations, and values—the culture—in which he or she was immersed during the first years of life.

Anthropological research goes on just about everywhere, including in societies that you might never have heard of such as Aka, Baka, Hadza, !Kung, Pirahã, Qashqa'i, Sámi, Yanomamö, and Tapirapé.[5] Among the societies receiving the most attention from anthropologists are the United States on the one hand, and the Chinese, Japanese, and Korean societies of East Asia on the other. Since the early 1970s, these research efforts have yielded literally hundreds of reports about children's learning and parental child-raising. My estimate is well over 500.

This was my raw material. The findings from this research enabled me to compare East Asia and the United States in terms of child-rearing and classroom learning. Surely there would be something of value for American education to be gained from this mountain of data. I decided to find out.

What I discovered is presented here in *The Drive to Learn*.

Cornelius N. Grove, Ed.D.
Brooklyn, New York
2017

Acknowledgments

My first "thank you" goes to my decades-long friend and professional colleague, Kay M. Jones, who edited and reedited drafts with her legendary eagle eye, did valuable background research that I hadn't even asked for, made innumerable valuable suggestions, and—with her longtime associate Anthony Pan—authoritatively advised me on the language and culture of China and Japan. As just one example, Kay's dogged investigation revealed that when parenting researchers referenced the Chinese word *guan*, they actually meant *guăn*, not *gūan*! Thank you, Kay!

Several friends and colleagues ably assisted me by commenting on drafts of the text and/or the online annotated bibliography. Unfailingly insightful from start to finish of the entire project was my business partner of 28 years, Willa Zakin Hallowell. Others who aided my efforts during portions of the project were Walt Beadling, Young Mi Park, Carolyn Feuille, and Stephanie Lisle. Whatever excellence this book might have is due, in part, to their advice and counsel.

During the writing of *The Drive to Learn*, I hoped to pay face-to-face visits to some of the scholars whom I had come to admire, and on whose work I was relying. To this end, I contacted several; two agreed. Thus, I came to spend a truly enjoyable two hours with Dr. Jin Li on the campus of Stanford University, and an equally enjoyable two hours with Dr. David F. Lancy at his home north of Logan, Utah. Jin and David, thank you for welcoming a complete stranger.

They are just two of the hundreds of anthropologists and kindred researchers from around the world whose perseverance yielded the findings on which this book depends. More than 100 of them are listed in this volume's bibliography, and hundreds more have contributed, and are still contributing, to the collective effort. All of them have my gratitude, respect, and admiration.

Introduction

Why have so many people been saying—for decades—that the outcomes of American education are poor? Because that has been the conclusion reached repeatedly by four types of measurement:

- the findings of researchers who spend time patiently observing inside American schools;
- the experiences of institutions that deal with recent high school graduates, such as colleges and employers, and with high school dropouts, such as the military;
- the performance of our students on domestic comparative tests such as the National Assessment of Educational Progress; and
- the performance of our students on international comparative tests such as the Program for International Student Assessment.

Those international comparative tests reveal that children in a few other nations *always* score at or near the top.[1] That's the main reason why Americans concerned about our "learning gap" often seek solutions by examining Finland, Poland, Singapore, China, Japan, and Korea.

Our attention to schooling in other nations has overwhelmingly been on the educators and policy makers there. When we seek solutions by looking at the practices of other nations, we ask the same kind of *adult-focused* questions that we always ask about education in our nation.[2]

A Fresh Approach to Seeking Solutions

This book takes a different approach. It doesn't pay any attention to adult educators and policy makers. Instead, it seeks solutions by looking at the children—especially at the younger children. This line of inquiry is supported by a mountain of data. We don't need to appropriate more funds for yet another research study. At least 500 studies have been carried out already.

So why aren't these findings a big part of our national conversation about children's learning?

First, these findings come from the field of anthropology.[3] Anthropologists focus on understanding the behavior and values of people living in a wide range of locations. Anthropology hasn't caught the public's attention like, say, cognitive psychology has. Anthropology studies people in groups. Americans are far more interested in learning about people as individuals. As for the anthropologists, most of them talk among themselves instead of talking with the rest of us.

Second—and as already noted—we Americans assume that all solutions to our educational problems will come when adult educators and policy makers change their inadequate practices. Explanations that point to the inadequacies of children simply don't gain traction with us.

But the anthropologists' findings about children's learning abroad are relevant to our search for solutions. Their findings should be part of our conversation about our children's poor learning.

The Drive to Learn summarizes, clarifies, and applies the findings of anthropologists and other social scientists, such as sociologists and interculturalists, using similar methods.

AN OVERVIEW OF HOW THIS BOOK PROCEEDS

Poor learning outcomes in American schools cannot be *totally* the fault of American educators. Our children are part of the problem, too. But how can we determine what our children's part is? One way is to compare them with other children whose learning in school is much better.

In order for such a comparison to be made, there must be a large and accessible body of research findings about *both* groups of children. As noted earlier, such findings exist. The other children are those who, between roughly 1970 and the early 2000s, were growing up in East Asia: China, Japan, and Korea. (Perhaps you think they're a bad choice because, "as everyone knows," Asian children just memorize and regurgitate. Try to keep an open mind.)

These findings reveal that those East Asian children were *highly receptive* to school learning. Compared with American children, they arrived at school more ready, willing, and able to learn in classrooms. Because they were *more receptive to learning*, they learned more.

Introduction xxi

In the following chapters, we'll embark on a step-by-step discovery process. We're not going to follow the researchers' progress year by year. Instead, we'll pose questions about the children of East Asia and discover what the researchers have found. Their answers will lead us to ask further questions, to which we'll discover further answers. After we have asked and answered questions nine times in a row, we'll emerge with a broad understanding of

- *why* those East Asian students were more receptive than American students to school learning,
- *how* the East Asian students became motivated to be highly receptive to school learning, and
- *what* American parents can do so that their children become more receptive to school learning.

THE PLAN OF THIS BOOK

The Drive to Learn includes nine chapters called "Discovery Steps," plus a chapter about what parents can learn from those discoveries, and another that addresses two related topics. At the end, there's a postscript, a non-annotated bibliography, and an introduction to the online annotated bibliography.

1. "Daring to Seek Answers" is the title of Discovery Step 1. Its opening question is: *Why do American students learn less than East Asian students?* We review the history of this concern by American citizens—and by a research team in Hong Kong. Back in the 1970s, that team decided to figure out why Chinese students, learning in old-fashioned ways, always scored higher than American students on the international comparative tests. At that time, much information about Chinese schooling was available from eyewitness reports of Westerners who had visited schools in China or even had taught there.
2. "Evaluating Eyewitness Reports" is the title of Discovery Step 2. Its opening question is: *What can we gain from Western reports about student learning in East Asia?* We must begin here because, as noted above, most information about East Asian schools came from Westerners who had *observed* East Asian classrooms—but who made little effort to explore beyond appearances. We'll examine the accuracy of two typical reports. In the end, we'll learn something important: East Asian students expect to gain understanding by investing a huge amount of time and effort in studying.

3. "Exploring Motivations" is the title of Discovery Step 3. Its opening question is: *What motivates students in East Asia to persevere in studying?* We will try to apply the concepts of intrinsic and extrinsic motivation to East Asian students, and we'll look at how they react to success and failure. We'll relate what we're discovering to the insights of American psychologist Carol Dweck. In the end, we'll learn that East Asian students have an internal determination or drive to persevere in learning, especially after a failure to learn.
4. "Analyzing Determination" is Discovery Step 4. Its question is: *Why is the determination to learn of East Asian students exceptionally strong?* We'll meet one of the researchers on whose work this book is based. She is Dr. Jin Li, a China-born American scholar who analyzed how Chinese and American students *think* about learning. Dr. Li tells us that, unlike American students, Chinese students are *emotionally driven to learn* because they associate learning with morality and virtue. This is an important fact but, so far, we have only a basic grasp of what it means. We need to learn more.
5. "Assessing Emotional Drive" is Discovery Step 5. It asks: *Why do East Asian students infuse learning with emotional drive?* This question brings us to probe the meaning of "self" in East Asia and the United States—is it just me, or is it *me and*? That leads us to explore research into the role of family in generating strong motivation to learn in children. We'll even look at findings that peer inside students' brains to reveal the strength of their family relationships. We'll learn that a millennia-old trait of the deeply unified East Asian family is an emotion-infused drive to learn. We need to discover more about its origin and nature. To do that, we'll need to think in new ways: first like a sociologist (step 6), then like a historian (step 7).
6. "Thinking like a Sociologist" is Discovery Step 6. Its question is: *Do sociological factors help explain East Asians' fervent drive to learn?* From an imaginary helicopter, we'll broadly consider two types of society—individualized and communitarian. In each, we'll explore how infants are raised so that they gain the skills they'll need to thrive as adults. The two child-raising methods differ in several ways and yield different outcomes. Communitarian societies ensure that one of the outcomes of child-rearing is that young children *learn how to be diligently receptive* to others who have already mastered whatever is to be learned.
7. "Thinking like a Historian" is Discovery Step 7. It asks: *Do historical factors help explain East Asians' fervent drive to learn?* We'll begin by finding that wherever schooling exists, children resist it. Two methods are used to counter their resistance: it can be *overcome* or *prevented*. To

Introduction   xxiii

reveal which method came to be used in the United States, and which in East Asia, we'll dig into history. As a result, we'll discover why American and East Asian families have different ways of life. In the ways of life of East Asians lies the answer to this book's main question, about why East Asian students are more receptive to school learning. It's time to turn our attention to those students' parents: how they think and what they do.

8. "Revealing How Parents Think" is Discovery Step 8. It asks: *What are East Asian parents' assumptions about how to raise children?* An East Asian family is deeply aware of its virtue or standing in the eyes of its community. The behavior of each family member, including each child, represents the family. So it is imperative that each child learns how to maintain the family's standing. Knowing that a child is malleable, her parents guide and shape her values, abilities, and social skills. They authoritatively mold her behavior. Their role is that of a coach and trainer. The role of American parents is more like that of a cheerleader.

9. "Revealing What Parents Do" is Discovery Step 9. It asks: *What are East Asian parents' approaches to coaching and training their children?* We'll look at common practices used by East Asian parents: (a) They maintain high expectations, often inching them even higher. (b) They govern their child's use of time, ensuring that most of it is dedicated to academic pursuits. (c) They're very generous in contributing their own time to serving as their child's coach. (d) They expect their child's self-esteem to grow as a result of goals attained. (e) They participate with their child, learning alongside him and jointly addressing challenges. (f) They directly shape, instruct, and train their child, focusing on how to accomplish tasks correctly.

10. "So What Should We Do?" is the first post-discovery chapter. It asks: *To what extent could—should—this new information change the way we do things?* First, it reports fresh research showing that the *critical thinking* ability of Chinese college freshmen *exceeds* that of American freshmen! What options exist for change? Ruled out as a realistic option is that American culture could be transformed. But it *is* realistic for a family's culture to be transformed. Such a change is challenging; a parent might reasonably decide not to attempt it. But for parents who wish to give it a try, this chapter offers "Seven Commitments to Your Child."

11. "Responsibility and Creativity" is the closing chapter, in two parts. The first asks: *Who is responsible for a student's learning?* This question is implied throughout the foregoing chapters; now we ask it directly. The answer for American education is very different from that for East Asian education, underscoring critical contrasts developed throughout this book.

The second part asks: *Why are East Asians believed to be less creative than Americans?* This question arises because whenever it's noted that our students learn less than East Asians, the knee-jerk response is, "But our students are *way* more creative!" The implication is that schools make people creative or not—an implication that we'll find to be too simplistic.

Two short sections round out this book:

1. The postscript is a discussion of two recent books on child-rearing by well-respected American scholars. One is by Alison Gopnik, a developmental psychologist. The other is by Robert A. LeVine and Sarah LeVine, a husband-and-wife team of anthropologists. Both books contend that American parents should stop trying so hard to ensure that their children turn out in certain ways—advice that seems at odds with the message here in *The Drive to Learn*.
2. "A Note about the Annotated Bibliography" is a description of what you can look forward to if you visit the online annotated bibliography, found on the Internet at www.thedrivetolearn.info.

ABOUT THIS BOOK

About the Research

The Drive to Learn relies on research. In fact, it relies entirely on research. But these pages were not written by a researcher (me) to communicate with fellow researchers. They were written by a concerned American (me) to communicate with you and other Americans in all walks of life.

This book doesn't simply repeat the researchers' findings. Rather, it tries to make their findings *understandable, easily remembered*, and *applicable*.[4] My goal is to weave a story using plain English, providing readily understandable explanations, and summing things up concisely.

Near the end of this book, you'll find a standard bibliography—that is, a list of my sources. And available as an aid to your fuller understanding, you'll find at www.thedrivetolearn.info something rare: an *annotated* bibliography of 100 of the research reports on which this book depends. For more information, see "A Note about the Online Annotated Bibliography" at the end of the book.

About the Use of Generalizations

An important goal of this book is to paint a Big Picture. It's a picture of the behavioral patterns and tendencies of people, considered in groups. To see the

Big Picture, we've got to go up in an imaginary helicopter and look down at large features of human experience. That misses details. But it also enables us to become aware of broad behavioral patterns and tendencies of groups.

To discuss those patterns and tendencies, we must speak in *generalizations*. Almost every paragraph of this book has at least one. Consider, "American children are less receptive to school learning." It implies that *every* American child has low receptivity. Of course, that's nonsense.

We all use generalizations constantly. We make statements about families, neighborhoods, age groups, sports teams, political parties, occupational groups, and such. We almost always do this without stopping to consider each separate individual in the group. But if someone calls this to our attention, in most cases we'll agree that *not every* group member is like that.

So why do we need to use generalizations? Because within each human group—family, village, corporation, ethnic group—behavior and values vary. Culture is about within-group *tendencies and trends*. Culture is not about identical copies. So in order to talk about the Big Picture patterns within any group, we must speak about *tendencies and trends*: generalizations.

About the Focus on Values

This book is about *values*. A value is a preference for one state of affairs over another. A value is about the importance or worth of an idea, object, or event, compared with possible alternatives.

If you prefer a cheeseburger to a green salad, you value the former more; it's more important to you to eat a cheeseburger (often if not necessarily always). If your extended family wants your daughter to become a professional instead of a receptionist, the family values the former more. The idea of attaining professional status is more important to your family than any alternative.

Values influence behavior minute by minute, year after year. Most likely, you'll order the cheeseburger. Most likely, your daughter will apply to graduate school. *Values explain why.*

Throughout childhood, each individual learns the values of the group in which she is growing up. She learns how those around her evaluate the relative importance of all sorts of objects, events, people, thoughts, and activities. In *most* cases, a child comes to have values similar to the values of those around her. Her set of values results from repeated exposure: observation, imitation, and deliberate teaching. Later in life, she can modify those values. She even can rebel against them.

Here's why values are important when we're thinking about education: Most parents want their children to learn school subjects well. Many American children don't. Many East Asian children do. Beginning around 1970, this fact drew the attention of anthropologists and similar researchers who wanted to understand *why*. Their efforts led them to consider East Asian *values*—the preferences and priorities of East Asian parents, which influenced their behavior as they raised their children. This book relates what was discovered about their values and behavior.

The anthropologists did not view East Asians as inherently superior. East Asians were studied solely because *in one way*—classroom learning—their children outperformed American children.

About the Focus on Culture

When people live in groups, they tend to share similar values, and thus similar patterns of behavior. The fact that these are similar is captured by "culture." To talk about a culture is to describe in a Big Picture way the patterns that have been observed within the group in question.

Note the word *similar*. Culture *never* means that everyone in a society is in unanimous agreement or has identical behavior. Some may opt out; others may innovate. But when *the majority of* people in a society choose *similar* ways of thinking, valuing, and doing, we speak of that society's culture. Any statement about a society's culture is necessarily a generalization.

Within these pages, the term "culture" will appear often, sometimes in the phrase "cultural values." This is because culture is very much about people's values, and about the behavior that results from their values. Culture doesn't cause behavior. *It describes what people care about and do*.

About the East Asians

Again and again in this book, you'll read that "East Asians do this" and "don't do that." East Asia is a region comprising China, Hong Kong, Taiwan, Japan, and Korea. In most cases, the languages spoken by their residents are not mutually intelligible. Each one has a culture with unique characteristics. And during recent centuries, the people living in these areas have often been on unfriendly terms. Wars have occurred, some within the bitter memories of people alive today! Given all these differences, why are East Asians often lumped together in this book?

There is agreement among anthropologists and other specialists that the values of East Asians share many fundamental similarities. For example, although research reveals differences in how parents throughout the regions named above relate to their children,[5] it also reveals striking parallels in how they think about parenting, early childhood, and children's learning.

My own experience as a reader of research reports is illustrative. Many well-respected anthropologists have looked at children and/or parents in China, Japan, and the United States. In most cases, the findings from these studies disclose similarities between the Chinese and Japanese subjects while significant differences separate those two from the American subjects.

Relatively little research has been done in Korea. So many of the generalizations that follow are based on studies carried out in the Chinese and Japanese communities of East Asia and, to a lesser extent, in immigrant Chinese and Japanese communities within the United States.

About the Time Frame

Most research on which this book relies was carried out after 1970. Much occurred between 1985 and 2000, when there was a surge of interest in children's learning in China and Japan, and to a lesser extent, Korea. Hundreds of research reports appeared. Some reports published after 2000 were based on research carried out during the 15-year surge.

Today, changes are underway in East Asia. The most prominent example is in China where, in response to the emerging knowledge economy, "Education for Quality" became government policy in 1999. Its goals were "fostering creativity and practical skills." Some claim that the new policy bears the fingerprints of Western liberal/progressive educators.[6]

But it's not the purpose of this book to compare American and East Asian education or child-rearing today. *Its purpose is to gain insight into why children have different levels of receptivity to school learning.* The research completed between the 1970s and early 2000s provides us with useful comparisons between children who were more, and less, receptive to school learning.

About the Use of Chinese Words

A handful of Chinese and Japanese words are included in the text. Each one's meaning is explained when it first appears.

The various dialects of the Chinese language include many homonyms, which are words that are pronounced similarly but have different meanings. (In English, an example is *aisle*, *isle*, and *I'll*.) All Chinese dialects are *tonal*: When spoken, the pitch or "pitch contour" of a word's sound distinguishes its meaning from that of other words that otherwise are pronounced the same. The *written* characters of two or more homonyms are almost always different. Virtually all authors writing in English about China do not include the tone marks. They should.

This book includes all tone marks. An example of why comes in chapter 8, where the term *guǎn* is introduced. If it had appeared as *guan* (no tone mark), a reader with facility in Chinese could easily assume that the word *guān* was intended (part of *guānxi*, a common Chinese term often translated as "relationship"). But *guǎn* (third tone) and *guān* (first tone) have completely different written characters. Most important for our purposes, *guǎn* and *guān* have subtly different meanings that turn out to be at the heart of what chapter 8 is trying to explain!

I know a handful of words in Chinese and none in Japanese. But I have two old friends and colleagues—Kay M. Jones and Anthony Pan—who are deeply versed in both languages as well as both cultures. They have not only helped me get the Chinese tones right, they've also advised me on many other cultural matters. In the notes, I signal their assistance like this: [KJ & AP].

Chapter One

Discovery Step 1: Daring to Seek Answers

Why Do American Students Learn Less Than East Asian Students?

The problem that we're thinking about isn't new.

Imagine yourself back in the mid-1960s. You're a parent of two children, one in junior high school and one beginning primary school. You're devoted to their getting a good education. You always show up for parent-teacher conferences, and you even attend some PTA events. OK, you never attended a school board meeting, but on a recent school bond referendum, you voted "yes."

One day a news item catches your eye.[1] It's about the First International Mathematics Study, which tested and compared the scores of students in 12 nations. Our American 13-year-olds scored next to last, just ahead of 13-year-olds from Sweden.[2] Our high school seniors scored dead last. Well, you say, those American losers weren't from our local schools!

You forget about this for a few years. After all, *your* two kids are doing pretty well in school. Then, a similar news item: The First International Science Study compared 10- and 14-year-olds and seniors in 11 nations. Our 10-year-olds came in second, behind the Japanese. Our 14-year-olds were in the middle of the pack. Our seniors? Dead last again. Does this mean, you wonder, that as American children advance through school, they fall further and further behind?

An editorial recalls Sputnik. You remember it, back in 1957. You carried your first child outside that evening and waited until a brilliant dot of light scooted across the sky. A man-made satellite! But you knew—the *world* knew—that this was not an American achievement. Russians put it up there. They had out-calculated and out-engineered us. Were our schools to blame?

Your older child makes it into college . . . where he has trouble keeping up. This, together with more news items, deepens your concern that all might not be well. There are more international tests. American students in their midteens *always* place near the middle; seniors *always* place at, or close to, the bottom. What is the explanation?

If an Unfriendly Foreign Power . . .

Now it's the 1980s. Depressing facts about American education are still in the news. Many colleges, for example, need to offer remedial courses to entering high school grads. A National Commission on Excellence in Education is appointed. Its report, *A Nation at Risk*, is phrased in terms that anyone can understand.[3]

> If an unfriendly foreign power had attempted to impose on America the mediocre educational performance that exists today, we might well have viewed it as an act of war. As it stands, we have allowed this to happen to ourselves.

A Nation at Risk gets your attention, and that of your education-minded friends. You all read and discuss whatever you can find about education. There's plenty to read! Much of it focuses on dismal facts about American students' learning in school. The facts come from four sources:

1. One comes from researchers who spent months patiently observing what actually is going on in schools and classrooms. What are students studying? How is their learning evaluated? What standards are being maintained? How is class time spent? Their reports reveal that most students are devoting astonishingly little time and effort to academic subjects.[4]
2. Another comes from organizations dealing with young people. Business leaders report that they have entry-level job openings but reject many applicants because they lack basic reading and math skills. The military services warn that they're turning away youth who want to enlist but don't know even simple things that they should have learned in school. And then there's all those colleges, expanding the seating capacities of their remedial courses.
3. A third set of disappointing facts comes from our domestic comparative test, the National Assessment of Educational Progress. NAEP tests students at the 4th, 8th, and 12th grade levels, then reports results for each state and for a variety of demographic groups.[5]
4. Finally, there are those international comparative tests, now called TIMSS and PISA.[6]

You and your friends realize that, even if those international comparative tests did not exist, you'd be worrying just as much about education. Entry-level jobs left unfilled? Kids who don't know enough to be a buck private? Remedial courses for last year's high school *graduates*?

What should everyone make of this? *Why are American students learning so little?*

THE QUESTION, RESTATED

Within our nation, there were plenty of organizations and individuals who were trying to figure out why American students were learning so little, and devising ways of bringing about change.

What no one knew was that a similar question was being asked on the other side of the world.

Outside the United States, the results from the international comparative tests were called "league tables" because, just as soccer leagues ranked their teams, these results ranked the students of various nations. Whenever the league table from the latest test was published, it was examined in every participating nation by educators and policy makers. Beginning in the 1980s, each new league table also was scrutinized by researchers at the University of Hong Kong.

Although Hong Kong hugs the coast of China, in those days it was a British colony. At the university there, the researchers who poured over each new league table were an international group, including several Australians. Their unit gathered information about education in various nations. It was called the Comparative Education Research Center (CERC).

CERC's lead researchers were Westerners. They had been impressed by a modern, Western teaching approach[7] that had gained adherents in Britain and America. Its key ideas were that

- the topics studied in classrooms should be selected to reflect the children's individual interests;
- how teachers teach should be shaped by the children's natural and preferred ways of learning; and
- each child's unique abilities and traits should be drawn out and encouraged to grow and flower.

These ideas guided choices. For example, modern-thinking educators demanded small class sizes so each child's unique traits could be drawn out, and teachers could give personal attention to every student. They had long claimed that these new methods would lead to superior learning.

The Same Outcome Again and Again

When the CERC researchers studied each new set of league tables, they noticed that the average scores of the American students were mediocre or worse—and that the average scores of Chinese, Japanese, and Korean students were at or near the top. Every time, every test.

That raised a question in the researchers' minds. Their question wasn't, "Why are American children learning so little?" After all, they were far away from the United States. Their university was located on the opposite side of the planet (on a clear day, you can *see* China from Hong Kong).

Instead, their question was guided by their professional field: *comparative* education. They asked a question that enabled them to do comparisons. Their question went something like this:

> How can it be that the old-fashioned teaching approaches used in China always get results that are far better than the modern approaches used in America?

It wasn't long before the group at CERC hit on a shorthand way of referring to their question. They called it "The Paradox of the Chinese Learner." In its simplest form, the paradox was stated like this: *How can outmoded learning methods lead to superior learning outcomes?*

THE PARTS OF THE PARADOX

Thinking about school learning was a full-time job at CERC. So it was easy for the staff to come up with examples of how Chinese and other East Asian students learn in school that were—as judged by modern Western educators—old-fashioned and incapable of yielding genuine understanding. In particular, Westerners had long criticized East Asian schools for the following reasons:

1. **Huge class sizes:** In China, class sizes were mind-numbingly high. In the primary grades, class sizes were rarely below 30. In high schools, class sizes of 50 or more were typical. So there was no possibility of a teacher's routinely attending to the needs of individual students.
2. **Passive students, authoritarian teachers:** Teachers above the primary grades gave every appearance of being inflexible authorities. Western visitors to Chinese classrooms often left in dismay about students sitting "passively" while the teacher "lectured." Students were never seen to ask a question, offer a comment—or even *answer* a question! Everything was

top-down. "Spoon-feeding" reigned. The students were "docile." The climate was "cold."
3. **Grueling examinations:** Teaching in China above the primary level was exam focused. The exams themselves, set by centralized authorities, were *far* more grueling than anything known to Americans. Gaining a top mark on these "external" exams was the goal of most Chinese students. They studied all the time. Westerners noted with alarm that the students were "extrinsically motivated."
4. **No opportunity to explore and discover:** Chinese teaching put emphasis on the basics, and on mastering them *first*. This up-front focus on basics led to what modern Western teachers viewed as collateral damage: no opportunity for young pupils to explore, discover, and have their own ideas; and many opportunities for them to imitate, practice, repeat, perfect—in a word, to drill. "Drill to kill," went the Western refrain, "is a *really bad* way to learn!"
5. **Rote memorization:** Worst of all, Chinese students *memorized* stuff! Just like "drill," "rote" was an ugly word to modern educators. Saying that a person was learning something "by rote" meant that they expected to "regurgitate" it on a test. Genuine understanding could not possibly result. Rote was—still is!—the learning method that Westerners love to hate.

So the question being asked by more and more Americans during the 1960s, 1970s, and 1980s—Why are American students learning so little?—became mirrored by the question asked at CERC in Hong Kong: How come old-fashioned teaching methods get better results than modern ones?

Imagine yourself again as that 1960s parent who was optimistic about the futures of her two children. It's the 1980s now; they're both starting their own families. Because you've come to care about American education—now as a grandparent—you're still drawn to reading anything you come across about educational research, reform efforts, and innovative teaching methods. What you read helps you believe that American students will soon improve. You want to believe!

But what you *never* read is any news item about the *comparative* studies being carried out by the researchers from the University of Hong Kong. As time passes, they are joined by dozens of other researchers from universities all over the world. Their quest to unravel "The Paradox of the Chinese Learner"—later changed to "The Paradox of the *Asian* Learner"—gradually brings a comprehensive perspective to the issue. For they are trying to understand, at the deepest levels, why East Asian students learn more than American students.

We will look over their shoulders as, step by step, they ask questions and discover answers.

REVIEWING STEP 1 OF THE DISCOVERY PROCESS

We've started the discovery process by recognizing that a problem exists. We have stated the problem as a question: *Why do American students learn less than East Asian students?*

Next, we need to consider where we might find information to help us answer that question—information about children's learning in both the United States and East Asia.

Many would say that we already know a great deal about children's learning in East Asia. A few pages back, we reviewed five widely reported observations about classrooms there: passive students, authoritarian teachers; no opportunity to explore and discover; drill to kill; rote . . .

Most of that information about East Asian education came from Westerners who visited East Asia to observe schools and classrooms there. In fact, some of them actually taught in schools and universities in East Asia. They were eyewitnesses! Can't we trust their reports?

Let's dare to seek answers by first carefully evaluating the answers we've grown accustomed to hearing. In step 2, "Evaluating Eyewitness Reports," we'll take the next step in our discovery process by asking, *What can we gain from Western reports about student learning in East Asia?*

FURTHER READING

If you'd like more detail about the researchers' findings, or simply wish to know what inspired the contents of Discovery Step 1, read the following entries in the annotated bibliography at www.thedrivetolearn.info.

- Biggs, John (2001). Teaching across cultures.
- Stevenson, Harold W., & James W. Stigler (1992). *The Learning Gap: Why Our Schools Are Failing and What We Can Learn from Japanese and Chinese Education.*
- Watkins, David (2000). Learning and teaching: A cross-cultural perspective.

Chapter Two

Discovery Step 2: Evaluating Eyewitness Reports

What Can We Gain from Western Reports about Student Learning in East Asia?

Students sitting "passively." Classrooms where "spoon-feeding" reigns. No opportunities for children to express *their* ideas; plenty of opportunities for them to "drill to kill." Evidence of extrinsic motivation everywhere. And, get this: The students actually *memorize* stuff!

These reports about East Asian children and classrooms came from eyewitnesses, people who, with their own eyes and ears, had *seen and heard* what they were talking about.

The accuracy of eyewitness testimony during trials came into doubt more than a century ago, after some suspected that innocent people were being wrongly convicted. But here's the thing: In those cases, the eyewitnesses were bystanders who fleetingly observed an event in progress.

The reports about schooling in East Asia are different. They came from people who devoted hour after hour to patiently observing—or even teaching—students in Japan, China, and Korea.

QUESTIONING THE EYEWITNESS REPORTS

At the Comparative Education Research Center, staff members were familiar with accounts of East Asians' classroom learning. They had collected many statements from Westerners. For example, here's how two Australian professors complained about their students there:[1]

> In my discipline, they all want to rote-learn material rather than think.

> It can be difficult to cope, in small (seminar) classes, with overseas students who are reluctant to discuss, criticize reading, and express an opinion.

In Hong Kong, Western professors also expressed frustration with Chinese students:[2]

> Hong Kong students display almost unquestioning acceptance of the knowledge of the teacher or lecturer. . . . [There's] an emphasis on strictness of discipline and proper behavior, rather than an expression of opinion, independence, self-mastery, creativity, and all-round personal development.

These comments came from people who were routinely teaching East Asians. What reason could possibly exist to question the accuracy of their reports that East Asians want to rote-learn rather than think, are reluctant to discuss and criticize, and put no emphasis on self-development?

At the Comparative Education Research Center, staff members decided that, actually, there were three good reasons to question such eyewitness testimony:

- Each of those statements contained someone's *judgment*, not a neutral description of behavior.
- The judgments were conclusions about other people's unseen *inner states* ("they are passive").
- Underlying the judgments were values and beliefs that the judges learned in a faraway land.

To discover how East Asians really go about learning, the researchers couldn't rely on these eyewitnesses. Instead, they needed to figure out what *behavior* led the Westerners to say those things. Then they needed to learn, from the East Asians' own perspective, *why* such behavior occurs.

Here's what the researchers discovered when they probed into two types of behavior that, for decades, had sparked criticism from Westerners: passiveness in class, and rote memorizing.

PASSIVENESS IN CLASS

No doubt about it: If you observe an East Asian classroom above the primary grades, you're going to see students sitting still, listening to the teacher, and poised to take notes. You'll almost never see them raising their hands, discussing in small groups, or even speaking out loud for any reason. One exception: you'll probably see them stand and formally greet their arriving teacher.

Neutral Descriptions

What you just read is a "neutral description." It describes *observable* behavior—they listen, take notes, greet, do not raise hands. No judgments. Nothing about unseen inner states.

If you've observed a scene such as the one described above, it's likely that, in talking with other Americans about it, you'll capture the essence of what you saw. If you say, "They're passive," your listeners will get it. So why plod through details such as sitting, listening, not raising hands, and such?

Here's why. "Passive" is something you cannot directly observe. It's a judgment about someone else's inner emotional state. If American students were behaving that way, you'd be on firmer ground to conclude, "They're passive." But now we're observing Asians in Asia. You'd be making a Made-in-the-USA judgment about Asian students' inner states. Not a good idea.

What *is* a good idea is to *neutrally* describe the scene, then wonder, "Why are the students behaving like that?" Maybe you'll figure out that, yes, they *are* passive. But maybe not.

What Does "Passive" Mean?

Let's begin with a small sample of how East Asian students themselves react to our judgment that they are "passive" in class. A Chinese student at a British university said:[3]

> We are active in our minds. We are thinking all the time. Our minds follow the lecturer with questions and challenges. We are just not used to speaking out. But all of us know very well what is going on and we know the answers to the questions those lecturers asked or other students raised.

An 8-year-old Chinese pupil said this to criticism that he was listening passively:

> I may be listening but I am not passive. I am learning in my head. I learn from my teacher. I also learn from what my friends do. If they make a mistake, I learn from that, too.

Two quotes prove nothing. But they do raise a question: What do we Americans mean when we say that someone is "passive"?

We mean *not visibly active*. One of our favorite edu-speak words is "engaged," meaning busy with activity. We expect to see verbally, sometimes even physically, active students in classrooms. Many American teachers give each student a grade for "class participation." The majority of East Asian students definitely would get an "F" for that!

What do East Asians expect from their students? *Mental engagement.* They think that rapt attention demonstrates mental engagement. Wondering, questioning, and trying to understand don't require out-loud verbal or physical activity. They *do* require attention and concentrated thought. On the surface, that looks "passive"—to an American.

We associate verbal and physical activities with learning. We expect to see students waving their hands, asking and answering questions, discussing ideas with classmates, and being busy in small groups. We even like to see them openly disagreeing with the teacher or the textbook.

Ask yourself this: Is it necessary for *all* such activities to occur *inside* classrooms?

What Happens *inside* Classrooms

Here and in East Asia, people view learning as occurring in two locations. One is in the classroom. The other is outside the classroom. But we and they view these two locations differently. We see the classroom as the place where all important learning activities occur. Outside the classroom is where homework occurs. In East Asia, in-class and out-of-class activities are equally important.

What happens in East Asian classrooms? The material to be learned is delivered to the students. That material—algebra, biology, history, whatever—is found in the textbook and in the teacher. Both are authorities. Classroom time is the opportunity for the students to receive the material from authorities: primarily from their teachers but also from the textbook authors.

To *receive* the material—and in the case of courses such as math and calligraphy, to practice it under the teacher's supervision. But not to discover or explore it. Not to ask questions about it. Not to discuss it in small groups. Not to fully understand it. Class time is precious because it's *when students receive knowledge from authorities*. Students don't want to sidetrack that process by asking questions, forming groups, sharing ideas, or any other distracting interruptions.

What happens in American classrooms? All of the above learning activities occur. Yes, the students receive the material, and in certain courses they practice it. In addition, they ask questions about it, discuss it in small groups, and offer their own ideas about it. Ideally, they explore it, make discoveries, and find applications. And a parallel goal is for each child to express his or her unique abilities and ideas. It's acceptable for them to do this by openly disagreeing with their teacher. After all, here in the United States teachers are not expected to be subject matter authorities.[4]

What Happens *outside* Classrooms

What happens outside East Asian classrooms? *Everything else.* Students read, practice, seek answers to questions, discuss the material, disagree with it in their minds and, in impromptu debates with fellow students, offer their own ideas, explore it further, make discoveries, and find applications. Students work with the material by themselves, with a friend, in larger groups, and even with the teacher. Their goal is to master the material—*outside* of class.

What happens outside American classrooms? Homework. This means practicing skills and reading. Occasionally it includes working on a project or reviewing for an exam. All those other learning activities? *Rarely* outside of class.[5]

Perhaps you're wondering how all those activities go on outside of class in East Asia.

The explanation is that outside-of-class contacts among students, and between them and their teachers, often are learning focused. For example, after class is dismissed, students with questions sometimes speak with the teacher just outside the classroom door. Equally likely is that students with questions will first go home and learn more about the topic. Then, outside of class, they'll approach the teacher not simply to get a question answered, but *to have an informed discussion* about the topic. In East Asia, teachers expect this.

Many students get together with other class members for the purpose of supporting each other's learning.[6] These study groups are student initiated; they are neither required nor suggested by their teachers. They occur at a wide variety of locations, most of them outside the school building. Here is where students ask questions, discuss the material, share insights from readings, and find applications. These get-togethers may be social, but their purpose is learning.

If you're thinking that all this outside-of-class learning activity is very time consuming, you are right. East Asian students spend their outside-of-class time quite differently from Americans.

The charts in figures 2.1 and 2.2 summarize this set of East-West differences.

ROTE MEMORIZING

Get an American talking about rote memorization and you'll hear that it's a load of boring effort that cannot lead to real understanding. The *Oxford English Dictionary* agrees: "rote" is "the mere exercise of memory without proper understanding of, or reflection upon, the matter in question."

What should happen *inside* classrooms?	
In East Asia	**In America**
Material to be learned is delivered to the students via textbook and teacher, sources viewed as authoritative. Students are expected to be *mentally* engaged: attentive, receptive, and thoughtful. They remain quiet and avoid all distractions and interruptions.	Material to be learned is delivered to the students via textbook and teacher, sources viewed as non-authoritative. The students are expected to be verbally, even physically, engaged in numerous activities: asking and answering questions, discussing, exploring, discovering, finding applications, etc. Students may disagree with the material and offer their own ideas. They should express their unique personalities and abilities.

Figure 2.1.

What should happen *outside* classrooms?	
In East Asia	**In America**
Homework, as in America. *And* asking and answering questions, discussing, exploring, disagreeing with the material, offering their own ideas, discovering, finding applications, etc. These activities occur in small study groups, *not required* by teachers, that many students join. Also, students may approach teachers with questions outside classrooms, including in the hallway right after class.	Homework: practicing skills and reading, sometimes also working on a project or reviewing for an exam. (The quantity of outside-classroom work is small by East Asian standards, and is gradually declining.)

Figure 2.2.

Well, it turns out that not only in the United States, but—believe it or not—*also in East Asia*, people agree that rote achieves merely an ability to "regurgitate" information on exams.

Is Memorizing Useful?

East Asians say that *rarely* is the goal of their studying to repeat from memory. Yet they often talk of memorizing. For them, rote and memorization are two different things. The challenge for the researchers was to figure out what East Asians have in mind when they talk of *memorizing*.

The belief that the students memorize great swatches of material came about because they could be seen going over and over *and over* material to be learned. To most Westerners, the students were rote memorizing. But, concluded the researchers, that's not accurate.

What's accurate is to understand their learning process as using a "repetitive strategy," also called a "rehearsal strategy." It is *step one* of East Asian students' pathway to thorough understanding.[7] The four steps of that pathway are . . .

1. **Repetition:** They repeatedly go over the material in an effort to recognize all the meanings it contains. This leads to at least partial memorization, and gradually shades into . . .
2. **Understanding:** They work at fully grasping the material's intention, style, and implications.
3. **Application:** They look for ways to use the material in situations where it can be beneficial.
4. **Modification:** They approach the material interactively. This final step can involve having doubts about it, seeing possibilities for improving it, or using it for self-development.

These steps can be compared with the process that actors use when getting ready for a new role. Obviously, they must begin by going over and over the script, resulting in their being able to repeat it from memory. That step merges with their pondering of the deeper meanings in the script and possible interpretations of it. Additional time and effort enables them to "become" the character whom they're portraying. And when confidently "in role," they might introduce interpretive flourishes in their delivery, or even modifications of the script.

One group of researchers set out to discover the concepts that students use when they think about memorization. Two emerged. One was "mechanical memorization," which was similar to what we call "rote." The other was "memorization with understanding," which meant that the students found memorizing to be effective in increasing their understanding. As one Chinese teacher put it, "It is not a simple repetition. Because each time I repeat, I would have some new idea of understanding, that is to say I can understand better."[8]

Learning Fast and Learning Slow

Asians' quest for thorough understanding comes with a personal cost. They expect to gain understanding *gradually*, which means that it involves perseverance and much time and effort.

American students expect to gain understanding quickly—and when they do, they often say they have grasped the material by means of their inborn "insight," "intuition," or "aptitude." This belief arises from Americans' assumptions about the impact, in each person's life, of the natural abilities with which he was born.[9] We'll have more to say about this later on.

The belief that East Asian students constantly rote memorize but understand very little is a stereotype. Stereotypes often have a toehold in observable facts. It's easy to find East Asians going over and over material to be learned. Seeing this, Americans jump to a conclusion: "Rote!"

This is why we needed curious researchers who patiently explored in ways that were longer, wider, and deeper. For when they did, they figured out that East Asian students use a "repetitive strategy" as *step one* in their gradual pursuit of understanding. By the time they've completed all four steps, they often have attained a thorough understanding—*mastery*—of the material.

The chart in figure 2.3 summarizes this set of East-West differences.

What is the purpose of memorizing?	
In East Asia	**In America**
Memorizing and rote are seen as *different*. Rote has very few uses while memorizing has many. As step one of their studying process, most students apply a "repetitive (rehearsal) strategy" that leads to partial or full memorization. Their many repetitions help to clarify the material's meaning, and gradually enable the students to fully grasp its intention, style, and implications.	Memorizing and rote are seen as *identical*. Most people view memorizing as useless because it does not yield real understanding, and as worse than useless because it's boring. But some view memorizing as useful in limited circumstances.

Figure 2.3.

HOW STEP 2 ADVANCED OUR DISCOVERY PROCESS

We began this discovery step by evaluating the judgments we usually hear about East Asian students and classrooms. By turning to the findings of researchers who have thoughtfully and patiently investigated how students in East Asia learn, we found that two common judgments are seriously in error: that they are passive in class, and that they merely rote memorize.

Beginning in this way advanced our quest for understanding in two respects:

- We set the tone for the rest of this book. We'll be *relying exclusively on the findings of anthropologists and other social scientists* who, over 40 years, have painstakingly studied all aspects of East Asian child-rearing, parenting, learning, and early childhood education.
- We discovered that East Asian students expect to gain understanding gradually by means of perseverance and huge amounts of time and effort. What motivates students in East Asia to persevere in studying? That is the question that we'll address in Discovery Step 3.

FURTHER READING

If you'd like more detail about the researchers' findings, or simply wish to know what inspired the contents of Discovery Step 2, read the following entries in the annotated bibliography at www.thedrivetolearn.info.

- Stevenson, Harold (1994). Moving away from stereotypes and preconceptions.

About Passiveness in Class

- Biggs, John (1996b). Western misperceptions of the Confucian heritage learning culture.
- Cortazzi, Martin, & Lixian Jin (1996). Cultures of learning: Language classrooms in China.
- Cortazzi, Martin, & Lixian Jin (2001). Large classes in China: "Good" teachers and interaction.
- Pratt, Daniel D., et al. (1999). Chinese conceptions of "effective teaching" in Hong Kong.
- Tang, Catherine (1996). Collaborative learning: The latent dimension in Chinese students' learning.

About Rote Memorization

- Biggs, John (1996a). Learning, schooling, and socialization: A Chinese solution to a Western problem.
- Helmke, Andreas, & Thi A.T. Vo (1999). Do Asian and Western students learn in a different way? An empirical study on motivation, study time, and learning strategies of German and Vietnamese university students.

- Kember, David (2016). Understanding and teaching the Chinese learner: Resolving the paradox.
- Lee, Wing On (1996). The cultural context for Chinese learners: Conception of learning in the Confucian tradition.
- Marton, Ference, et al. (1996). Memorizing and understanding: The keys to the paradox?

Chapter Three

Discovery Step 3: Exploring Motivations

What Motivates Students in East Asia to Persevere in Studying?

Several years ago, my business partner and I became acquainted with an eminent management professor.[1] We were especially impressed with a pearl of wisdom we learned from him. He took a maxim of education—"Motivation breeds success"—and flipped it to become "Success breeds motivation." His maxim seemed to express something we'd learned in life.

"Motivation breeds success" is a time-tested principle because, as every teacher knows, the key to successful learning is *the student's motivation*. That's why every lesson plan needs to begin with something—anything—that is likely to arouse the students' interest in the lesson. Administrators, too, can play a role; useful techniques are described in the 2004 book, *101 Stunts for Principals to Inspire Student Achievement*.[2]

There's no mystery about students' needing motivation; they're just being human. But what are those *East Asian teachers* doing? Do they know something about motivating students that we don't? What can we learn from exploring how East Asian students become motivated?

"Intrinsic" and "Extrinsic" Motivation

Anyone who explores motivation learns that there's Good Motivation, and there's Not-So-Good Motivation. Let's think about Suzy, a student. Good Motivation is when "*Suzy* wants to . . ." Not "teacher wants Suzy to . . ." and not "parents want Suzy to . . ." And definitely not "threats drive Suzy to . . ." The Good Motivation type is "intrinsic." That's edu-speak for "coming naturally from within." Intrinsic motivation means that *Suzy herself* wants to learn.

Not-So-Good Motivation—such as "*parents* want Suzy to . . ." and "*threats* drive Suzy to . . ."—is "extrinsic," edu-speak for "coming from the outside." Someone or something else is pushing or enticing Suzy to get down to the work of learning when, really, she'd rather not.

The professor's flip—success breeds motivation—offers a different perspective on the matter. He's noting that success feels so good that we're motivated to attain it again, along with those good feelings that success brings. That's why businesspeople who need employees to get big projects done often arrange for them to enjoy "early wins."

It comes down to this: A big key to successful learning is intrinsic motivation. Successful learning breeds intrinsic motivation to strive to learn more. A responsibility of every teacher is to discover and liberally apply whatever intrinsically motivates each of her students. Correct?

Absolutely! Here in the United States, it's all correct. In East Asia? *None* of it is correct.

THE AGONY OF DEFEAT

The opposite of success is failure, defeat. That leads to agony, or at least disappointment—and *that*, as teachers know, reduces motivation. It works like this: If you fail, you're disappointed, possibly embarrassed. Your self-esteem suffers. You don't want to feel that way again. So your earlier motivation to try to learn the material is lowered, maybe even eliminated. Correct?

Here we go again: In the United States, correct. In East Asia, not correct. But perhaps you don't know why things are different here and there. It's a fascinating world-turned-upside-down story.

Through observation and interviewing, researchers from the Comparative Education Research Center (CERC) and other universities figured out that East Asians react to success and failure differently from us. With our typical hype, we talk about "the thrill of success; the agony of defeat." In East Asia, it's pretty much the opposite: success is nothing to get excited about. Failure? Now *that's* worth our attention!

Success and Failure in East Asia

In East Asia, failure gets more attention than success. It's not that success is bad; not at all! It's good; Asians smile . . . inwardly. But success also has a couple of downsides. It *could* lead one to gloat—Not Good in a society that values modesty and humility. And for East Asians, success isn't very *useful*. It tells them how far they've come and where they are now. But it doesn't tell them where they should be going next or give them information about how to improve further.

Look at it from an East Asian student's perspective. If I'm trying to master difficult material, a test will tell me how far I've come in learning it. If I do well on the test, that's good . . . but that was expected. I studied hard; so it's no big deal that I aced that test.

If I do poorly on that test, that's . . . well, disappointing. No reason to smile. But exactly *what did I not understand*? Whatever the answer, it's useful. It tells me what I need to do now to totally "get" the material. Failure points me to where and how to direct my study efforts.[3]

That's how East Asians, including children, think about success and failure. Failure gets more attention than success because it's more useful in directing one's self-improvement.

This is important: In East Asia, *an individual's ultimate goal is self-improvement.*

Because an East Asian student's goal is self-improvement, gauged by her mastery of the material, failure doesn't lower her motivation. Just the reverse! With the new information, her efforts have clearer goals. When she takes action—persevering hard work—to eliminate her weaknesses, her self-esteem goes up. Striving to improve herself is what her parents and teachers expect; it's what they all support; and it's what they all admire.

Not surprisingly, striving to improve is what she admires in herself.

Success and Failure in America

The researchers found that, in the United States, success gets more attention than failure. Success is great! You receive open praise or approving smiles from your teachers and parents. (Your friends? Let's not go there now.) Your inborn strengths are confirmed. Your self-esteem gets a boost or is maintained at its usual lofty level. Your motivation to work at the same task, or a similar one, goes up; doing it again will show off your strengths again. As the old saying goes, "Nothing succeeds like success." And as the professor said, "Success breeds motivation."

Failure? Not good. Praise is scarce. Approving smiles are forced. Your self-esteem takes a blow because one of your inborn weaknesses is exposed for all to see. Your earlier motivation to work at this challenging task, or a similar one, is lowered because that weakness might be put on display a second time. For American students, it's hard to find an upside to failure.

American students and their parents pay little attention to failure. We're not talking about anything so extreme as being "in denial." The failure *is* acknowledged. Very often, though, a reason is found to show that the failure *is not due to an inborn weakness of the student*. Typical reasons are that he was ill, or the test was unfair, or the testing conditions were poor, or the Big

How do students react to *successful* learning?	
In East Asia	**In America**
Success is good, but it doesn't receive much attention. Success was the intended outcome, so usually it's not a surprise. It has little effect on self-esteem. Success isn't useful because it doesn't reveal any critical weaknesses. It doesn't point the way for further self-improvement.	Success is very good, very desirable, and it receives a lot of attention. It is openly admired by parents and teachers. Success is useful because it reveals or confirms one's inborn strengths. It boosts one's self-esteem, or maintains one's already high self-esteem. Success motivates a student to continue working at the same or similar tasks.

Figure 3.1.

How do students react to *unsuccessful* learning?	
In East Asia	**In America**
Although failure is disappointing, it doesn't lower self-esteem. It *does* get attention. It is useful because it reveals weaknesses and points the way to self-improvement. Self-esteem, and esteem in the eyes of others, goes up when one works long and hard to eliminate weaknesses. Consequently, one's motivation to persevere is heightened.	Failure is disappointing, so it doesn't get much attention. It lowers one's self-esteem because it reveals weaknesses and thus casts doubt on one's inborn capabilities. One's motivation to persist at the challenging task is lowered. Reasons may be given to show that the failure isn't due to inborn weakness.

Figure 3.2.

Game was occurring later that day. Or he might admit that he didn't study quite hard enough.

The charts in figures 3.1 and 3.2 summarize this set of East-West differences.

WHY MOTIVATIONS DIFFER

In the previous section, the word "inborn" appeared several times. The term "inborn" holds a clue to the mystery of why we Americans are motivated so differently from East Asians. Exploring this mystery takes us even further into the amazing story of how East Asians think about learning.

Decades ago, anthropologists figured out some things about Americans. Like people in every other society, we Americans have our own characteristic ways of thinking about children and their learning. Typically, we believe that each newborn baby arrives with a unique set of inborn abilities—*and* that those abilities are fixed and stable. "Fixed and stable" means that

- each ability arrives in a certain amount (high, medium, or low), which is its *potential*.
- each ability needs development so its potential can be reached; this is the job of schools.
- development is unlikely to enable any ability to expand beyond its inborn potential.[4]

An American Psychologist Weighs In

Imagine yourself in the shoes of two American students, Andy and Betsy. (By the way, the word "assume" will now be in use, meaning "take for granted, believe subconsciously.")

First, you're Andy: You assume that your abilities were given to you at birth in amounts that are fixed and stable. They add up to your potential. They are what you've got to work with, no less, no more. In terms of everyday living, you have good reason to believe that you're pretty smart. Then one day, you score poorly on a big test. How are you likely to react?

Now be in Betsy's shoes: You know that you were born with certain abilities, but you *don't* assume they're fixed. Those abilities were the ones you *started with*, and you assume that they can be developed and expanded. In terms of everyday living, you have good reason to believe that you're pretty smart. Now you, too, score poorly on that big test. How do *you* react?

This question has interested researchers, including many psychologists. One of them has become very well known among educators. She is Carol S. Dweck of Stanford University.[5]

Dweck and her colleagues found that, among American children, the assumptions some make are like Andy's, while the assumptions others make are like Betsy's. They gave names to these assumptions: Andy has a "fixed mindset." Betsy has a "growth mindset."

If, above, you imagined yourself in the shoes of Andy and Betsy, compare your reactions with those that Dweck and her colleagues found again and again among American schoolchildren:

- FIXED MINDSET: Those who think like Andy, when facing failure, are disappointed—and embarrassed. Andy had been holding himself up as smart,

but the test score showed that he is not *that* smart. If you're a fixed-mindset person like Andy, *it's very important for others to believe you're smart*. So when you get a low test score, which publicly casts doubt on your smartness, your motivation to devote more effort to studying that material is reduced. After all, *if you assume your abilities are fixed, more study can't make a difference.* A good strategy is to try to avoid this and other situations in which your lack of smarts might be publicly revealed.
- GROWTH MINDSET: Those who think like Betsy, when facing failure, are disappointed but not embarrassed. A setback such as scoring poorly on a test is viewed by them as a challenge. And—here's the critical difference—they assume that they can overcome that challenge *through their own perseverance and hard work*. That will expand their abilities. Their motivation to study harder is high; they assume that doing so *can* make a difference.

When Dweck and her colleagues look *only* at Americans, they find some who have a fixed mindset (like Andy) and some who have a growth mindset (like Betsy). So within our nation, people have a range of assumptions about their own abilities.

But when anthropologists *compare* Americans with East Asians, they find that, on the whole, Americans are more likely to assume that they were born with fixed abilities.

What Anthropologists Have Found

When anthropologists study East Asians, they find that most of them have very little interest in whether they arrived at birth with this or that "inborn" ability. Instead, they assume that their inborn abilities are flexible, capable of growth and expansion.

This is why the term "inborn" holds a clue to the mystery of why we are motivated so differently from East Asians. We assume inborn abilities affect children's school success. *East Asians don't.*

When discussing Americans' assumptions about a person's abilities, anthropologists use the word "fixed." That's the same word Dweck uses in talking about people like Andy. But when anthropologists discuss East Asians' assumptions about a person's abilities, they don't use Dweck's word, "growth." Instead, they usually say "malleable."

The word "malleable" comes from metallurgy. It means "able to be hammered or pressed permanently out of shape without breaking or cracking." The change in shape does not come easily. Effort, often lots of it, must be applied. The word "malleable" will appear often in the following pages.

Underlying Differences

We began by asking, "What motivates students in East Asia to persevere in studying?" Numerous studies have confirmed that . . .

- In East Asia, failure motivates students to try harder. The reason, in part, is that inborn abilities don't concern East Asians. They assume their abilities are malleable, so that trying harder *will* make a difference. Their goal is *high learning mastery*—again and again.[6]
- In the United States, failure discourages students from trying harder. The reason, in part, is that inborn abilities *do* concern Americans. They assume that those abilities are fixed, so that trying harder is unlikely to make a significant difference. But high (inborn) abilities are admired by others, who largely judge one's level of (inborn) ability by his level of performance. So the goal for American students is to publicly demonstrate *high learning performance*—again and again.

One anthropologist who studied these differences remarked that East Asians emphasize *self-improvement* while Americans emphasize *self-enhancement*.[7] The former is about increasing one's knowledge. The latter is about increasing one's standing in the eyes of other people.[8]

HOW STEP 3 ADVANCED OUR DISCOVERY PROCESS

We wanted to understand what motivates students in East Asia to persevere in studying. So we explored research findings about differences in the motivations of East Asian and American students. We've come to understand that East Asians seem inwardly determined to study long and hard. The characteristics of their inner determination or drive are as follows:

- It is not undermined by failure to learn; on the contrary, it's strengthened after a failure.
- It is not associated with an assumption that, at birth, one receives unique, fixed abilities.
- It's highly similar to what American psychologist Carol S. Dweck calls a "growth mindset."
- It shows up in individual East Asians as a consistent commitment to self-improvement.

East Asians are *inwardly determined* to persevere in studying. That raises an important new question: *Why* is their determination or drive to learn amazingly strong? On to Discovery Step 4.

FURTHER READING

If you'd like more detail about the researchers' findings, or simply wish to know what inspired the contents of Discovery Step 3, read the following entries in the annotated bibliography at www.thedrivetolearn.info.

- Chen, Chuansheng, & David H. Uttal (1988). Cultural values, parents' beliefs, and children's achievement in the United States and China.
- Chen, Chuansheng et al. (1996). Academic achievement and motivation of Chinese students: A cross-national perspective.
- Heine, Steven J., et al. (2001). Divergent consequences of success and failure in Japan and North America: An investigation of self-improving motivations and malleable selves.
- Hess, Robert D., & Hiroshi Azuma (1991). Cultural support for schooling: Contrasts between Japan and the United States.
- Li, Jin (2012). *Cultural Foundations of Learning: East and West*. See especially chapter 6.
- Mangels, Jennifer A., et al. (2006). Why do beliefs about intelligence influence learning success? A social cognitive neuroscience model. (Carol S. Dweck is one of this article's coauthors.)
- Ng, Florrie Fei-Yin, et al. (2007). European American and Chinese parents' responses to children's success and failure: Implications for children's responses.
- Salili, Farideh (1996). Accepting personal responsibility for learning.
- Singleton, John (1989). *Gambaru*: A Japanese cultural theory of learning.

Chapter Four

Discovery Step 4: Analyzing Determination

Why Is the Determination to Learn of East Asian Students Exceptionally Strong?

Jin Li [pronounced *Gin Lee*] was a girl growing up in China when the Cultural Revolution began in 1966. The next 10 years witnessed unparalleled upheaval throughout all sectors of society, and for countless individuals—one of whom was Jin Li. Together with 16 million other young Chinese, she was taken from her parents, "sent down" to the countryside, and ordered to do farm labor so she'd learn from the peasants and become "reeducated." Schools were shuttered across the nation.

She still was laboring on a farm and serving as a "barefoot doctor" in 1977,[1] when the revolution was declared at an end. At that time, Jin Li was the right age to enter university, and the universities were in the process of being reopened. Along with millions of others her age, she was urged to review her prior studies and take the first university entrance examination. She passed the exam, one of 4.7% of those tested.[2]

Jin Li was assigned to study German in Guangzhou. She plunged into her studies alongside her fellow students. An American who was teaching at Jin Li's college wrote that he "had never—and has never since—seen such a sight [libraries packed with students focused on studying] on any of the campuses of some twelve American colleges and universities where he had taught."[3]

FROM CHINA TO AMERICA

Jin Li fell in love. The lucky guy was that American who had come to teach at her college. After a year, he yearned for home. Jin Li, now a teacher of German, was eager to accompany him, but her English was abysmal. After arriving in Burlington, Vermont, her employment options narrowed to two: work as a restaurant kitchen aid or register as a substitute German teacher.

Unfortunately, Jin Li's first call to substitute was for an English teacher. She protested to no avail; she was needed. The administrators reassured her, saying it would be an easy job; all she needed to do was follow the absent teacher's lesson plan and "keep the kids out of trouble."[4]

> "What trouble?" I said to myself, gazing around. I had never seen, not even in my dreams, such a school, with all the brightly lit classrooms, hallways, and all the books in the library. The students [projected] self-confidence and happiness. This is a learning paradise! What trouble could there be for such blessed lives?
>
> To my shock, those students chatted freely and giggled and threw things at each other as if I, the teacher, did not exist. What struck me most was that they were not the least bit interested in learning the content of the already minimal English tasks.

An Awakening in America

Jin Li moved to Pennsylvania, where she taught German while attending the University of Pittsburgh. One of her courses concerned how to develop children's creativity. Captivated, she decided to study creativity further, and went to Harvard because Howard Gardner was on the faculty. There, she plunged into her studies again. "Finally and inevitably," she recalls . . .[5]

> I encountered *culture* as a developmental concept. I realized that I had been blind to culture. Once discovered, I could not see the world without it. Together with our biology, culture produces us, but we also alter culture continuously. *This interactive process is the inescapable force underlying child development.*

Jin Li's awareness of culture drew her interest to the subtle differences in how Chinese and American children are raised. It brought to her mind the voices of her parents as they instructed her about the importance of learning. They often repeated old Chinese maxims such as[6]

- Continue studying without respite, instruct others without growing weary.
- To know what you know and know what you do not know—this is wisdom.
- Learn, then you will know your inadequacy.

As well, Jin Li recalled her prerevolution years in Chinese elementary schools. After an exam, her teachers would single out a pupil to receive applause; *not* the one with the highest grade, but the one who had worked the hardest. When a pupil didn't do well, her teachers would point out that she hadn't listened well in class, hadn't concentrated, or hadn't practiced nearly enough. And never, *ever*, was a pupil's low grade assumed to result from her lack of inborn abilities.[7]

So what would *you* do if (a) you must select a research topic for your doctorate in education, (b) you'd recently become captivated by the power of culture to shape children, and (c) during much of your life you'd *lived* the differences in how Chinese and Americans think about learning?

It's no surprise that Jin Li selected a topic that enabled her to dig deeper into the differences in how Chinese and American cultures shape the ways their children think about learning.

A Research Project Is Prepared

Jin Li decided to explore what "to learn" and "learning" mean to people raised in the United States and China. As the equivalent Chinese word, she selected *xúexí* [pronounced *shwayshi*], which is translated as "to learn, to study" or "learning, studying." What comes into the minds of Chinese when they hear *xúexí*? What comes into the minds of Americans when they hear *to learn* or *learning*?

Through a process involving university students in the United States and China,[8] Jin Li came up with two very long "initial lists" of words and phrases. After the weak items were removed, her final "core lists" numbered 225 items for *xúexí*, 203 for learn/learning.

With these lists, Jin Li felt confident that she'd be able to figure out why, in comparison with Americans, Chinese students' determination or drive to learn is so exceptionally strong.

DEEP MEANINGS OF *LEARNING*

Jin Li already had discovered something useful. When the two initial lists had been finalized, she examined them carefully. Being Chinese, she wasn't surprised to find that, among the 478 Chinese words and phrases, there were many about working hard to learn, and about learning throughout one's entire life. But Jin Li was astonished to find, among the 496 English words and phrases, *none* about working hard to learn, and *none* about learning throughout one's life.

Examples of Chinese items about working hard included "Take great pains to study," "Do the utmost to self-study," "Diligent in one's learning," and "Learn assiduously [meticulously]."

Examples of Chinese items about lifelong learning included "Keep on learning as long as you live," which was the most often mentioned of all 478 Chinese items.

What the "Core Lists" Revealed

Jin Li focused her analysis on the two, shorter, core lists. Striking differences between the two lists emerged, summarized by figure 4.1:[9]

Characteristics of two core lists of terms related to *learning*	
Among the 225 Chinese words/phrases	**Among the 203 English words/phrases**
1. Many mentions of hard work, diligence	1. No mention of hard work or diligence
2. Several mentions of life-long learning	2. No mention of life-long learning
3. Very few mentions of thinking processes	3. Many mentions of thinking processes
4. Multiple words, lengthy expressions	4. Single words, common words
5. Several Chinese proverbs about learning	5. No American proverbs about learning
6. Many items refer to emotional drive	6. No item refers to emotional drive
7. Many items are "calls to action" to learn	7. No item is a "call to action" to learn

Figure 4.1.
Source: Jin Li (2012) *Cultural Foundations of Learning: East and West.* Based loosely on Table 3.2, page 81.

The 18 most-mentioned items in each list are found in figure 4.2.[10]

After Dr. Li—let's refer to her this way now—had examined the two core lists, she figured out that Americans and Chinese think about learning differently—*very* differently. She created two "models of learning," American and Chinese. Each model posed four questions[11]:

- What is the purpose of learning?
- How does one get learning done?
- What outcomes does learning bring?
- What emotions are associated with learning?

Using these questions, we'll explore Dr. Li's main discoveries. To do that, we'll consider responses written by an imaginary first-year college student in each culture.[12] Our American student in the United States will be *Andrew*. Our Chinese student in China will be *Chunli*.

Top 18 most-often-mentioned items in each core list	
Top 18 on the Chinese list	**Top 18 on the American list**
1. Keep on learning as long as you live	1. Study
2. Read extensively	2. Thinking
3. Learn assiduously	3. Teaching
4. Read books	4. School
5. Diligent in one's learning	5. Education
6. Extensive knowledge and multifaceted ability	6. Reading
7. Study	7. Teacher
8. Make a firm resolution to study	8. Books
9. Study as if thirsting or hungering	9. Critical thinking
10. There is no boundary to learning	10. Brain
11. Concentrate on learning	11. Discovery
12. Eager to learn	12. Understand
13. Take great pains to study	13. Information
14. Seek knowledge	14. Knowledge
15. The learned understand reasoning	15. Motivation
16. Study abroad	16. Library
17. Do one's utmost to self-study	17. Students
18. Learning without thinking is labor lost; thinking without learning is perilous [Confucius quote]	18. Learn by doing

Figure 4.2.
Source: Jin Li (2012) *Cultural Foundations of Learning: East and West*. Based on Table 3.1, page 80.

What Is the Purpose of Learning?[13]

Andrew's answer to this question would go like this: "The world I'm growing up in is complex. I need to be able to understand how it works if I'm going to go on to a satisfying career. Sure, I have potential. But if I'm going to reach my goals, I need to develop the abilities I have."

Chunli's answer would emphasize other themes: "I need to become as perfect a human being as possible so that I fit in with the world I'm growing up in. The knowledge I gain in college will enable me to do that, so it's important that I struggle to master it. Cultivating myself in this way will enable me to solve my own problems, advance my career, contribute to the welfare of others, and improve the standing of my family within its circle of friends and relatives."

For Andrew, knowledge is emotionally neutral. If he gains knowledge, it's likely to become useful to him. He talks of developing his inborn abilities so he can understand how the external world works and attain his personal goals within it. Andrew's focus is self-serving and *practical*.

For Chunli, knowledge is emotionally charged; it's linked with virtue, both personal and social. So she talks of *mastering* her studies to *perfect* herself and thus become self-sufficient and able to support others' well-being. Chunli's focus is self-serving and *moral*—moral because learning is about becoming a good human being in the eyes of others *and* a contributor to their welfare.

The Chinese know that learning has practical worth, but that isn't emphasized. Emphasized instead is learning's connection with morality, and with being a valued, contributing member of one's family and community. It's *that* connection that makes learning *emotionally* motivated.

How Does One Get Learning Done?[14]

Andrew would answer something like this: "I need to be *involved* with whatever I'm learning. As they say, 'Learn by doing!' Reading and listening are OK, but they're boring. I need to be *active* with whatever I'm learning. I need to take it apart and analyze it, or make a model of it, or find out how to use it. I'll come up with questions, or maybe I'll even doubt what I was told at first. I'll discover answers by getting input from the web, or my fellow students, or my teachers, or by reading more. Active steps such as these will enable me to learn to the best of my ability."

Chunli would answer something like this: "It's important for me to make an earnest, sincere effort to master whatever I'm studying. After all, gaining knowledge contributes directly to my excellence as a human being. So I'll be diligent and conscientious in my studies, not quitting or flagging if the going gets tough. I'm not as smart as some of my fellow students, but no matter! My own effort, perseverance, and concentration will make the difference. I'll end up with the same or better intellectual abilities as they, the same capacity to contribute to others."

These answers illustrate two huge differences between American and Chinese students, which go far in explaining why Chinese students' drive to learn is exceptionally strong.

The first concerns how people think about the relationship between ability and effort:

- Americans assume that (inborn) ability guides *and constrains* what their effort can achieve.

- Chinese assume that effort guides *and attains* the abilities that they're striving to achieve.

Americans assume that (inborn) ability places a ceiling—one's "potential"—on how much can be gained by studying. Studying harder is unlikely to crack through that ceiling.[15] Chinese assume that studying harder *can determine how high the ceiling eventually reaches.*

The second difference concerns how people think about the activities of learning:

- Americans view learning as a task to be done. They get it done using a step-by-step process that involves their minds and, ideally, physical activity and written and/or spoken dialogue.
- Chinese view learning as a virtue to be acquired. They acquire virtue in two ways: by mastering the knowledge and, in order to master it, by studying long and hard—which itself is virtuous.

Dr. Li found that this task/virtue difference can be detected in youngsters as young as ages 4, 5, and 6.[16] Her research demonstrated that young Americans viewed learning as a task to be accomplished; young Chinese viewed learning as gaining virtue while behaving virtuously. One of the Chinese 5-year-olds was asked if she liked a short story character, "Little Bear," who gave up after trying to learn how to catch fish. The child said no, and was asked why not:

Child: "[Little Bear] does something and stops halfway; she's got three hearts and two minds" [an old Chinese saying about absence of concentration].

Interviewer: "What's wrong with having three hearts and two minds?"

Child: "You do this thing for a while, then you switch to another thing for a while. You don't even pay attention. You can't learn good, and that's not good."

What Outcomes Does Learning Bring?[17]

Andrew would be likely to answer like this: "Understanding how the world works is the outcome I want. It's about knowing facts, and it's also about understanding their underlying principles. Deeper understanding should give me skills to solve problems and have my own insights and ideas, rather than accepting what others say. I want to be creative and I want to think critically. In these ways, learning should enable me to attain my full potential, to be the best I can be."

Chunli's answer would sound like this: "The outcome I'm studying for is knowledge that's broad and deep, and that I've fully mastered. I'll put it to use in my own daily life, and I'll use it to make contributions to the welfare of my family and friends. Knowledge enables me to perfect myself, to fit in with others, and to advance my career and, thereby, the standing of my family. So I expect to continue striving to gain and use knowledge throughout my entire life."

Andrew emphasizes his own mental skills, including creativity, critical thinking, and "not merely [accepting] what others say," which will help him reach his full potential. He doesn't talk of personal perfection, contributing to the welfare of others, or lifelong learning—outcomes foreseen by Chunli. Chunli doesn't talk of personal insights, creativity, or critical thinking. She doesn't imagine an outcome that's limited or constrained by her inborn mental potential.

What Emotions Are Associated with Learning?[18]

Here's how Andrew might respond: "If I'm learning something that's interesting or that I'm curious about, then it's fun and I'll put time into it. Another thing that gets me going is finding a good reason to challenge some expert, or having an insight that no one else thought of. And if I ace a test, that's great! But let's face it, teachers expect us to learn some stuff that's boring. They *tell* us why it's important. But if it doesn't grab my interest, I won't study it very much."

Here's how Chunli might reply: "When I was very small, my parents and relatives guided me to love learning, and taught me how to commit myself to learning. I have such deep respect for teachers and others who have more knowledge than I, who are better people than I. I want to hear what they have to tell me. I'm determined to correct my inadequacies under their guidance."

These two responses could hardly be more distinct. Chunli's helps us understand something that came up in step 3 of our discovery process. We reviewed two types of motivation, "intrinsic" and "extrinsic." In the 1990s, researchers began to doubt that those Made-in-the-USA terms apply in East Asia.[19] Chunli's statement illustrates why they doubted. So if we want to know why East Asian students study long and hard to the point of mastery, the answer won't be that they're motivated like Americans. The answer is going to be something completely different.

HOW STEP 4 ADVANCED OUR DISCOVERY PROCESS

Our initial question was why East Asian students' determination to learn is exceptionally strong. For answers, we relied on the research of Dr. Jin Li, who discovered that American and Chinese students think in distinctly different ways about learning. Her findings boil down to this:

- *What is the purpose of learning?* Americans learn for emotionally neutral, *practical* reasons. Chinese learn for an emotionally charged, *moral* reason: to become a virtuous human being.
- *How does one get learning done?* Americans, assuming that inborn abilities constrain their learning, approach it as a practical task. Chinese, assuming that their effort will enhance their inborn abilities and that learning increases their virtue, invest emotional drive in their learning.
- *What outcomes does learning bring?* Americans expect greater cognitive skill and creativity. Chinese expect greater personal perfection and ability to contribute to the well-being of others.
- *What emotions are associated with learning?* If a topic is interesting to an American, he can become emotionally engaged in pursuing it. From infancy, Chinese are taught how to learn, to revere learned people, and to feel that learning increases their personal and social perfection, which all combine to invest their learning efforts with *enduring emotional energy and drive*.

We need to know more about the emotions driving East Asian learning. We especially need to figure out *why* East Asians infuse learning with emotional drive. On to Discovery Step 5.

FURTHER READING

If you'd like more detail about the researchers' findings, or simply wish to know what inspired the contents of Discovery Step 4, read the following entries in the annotated bibliography at www.thedrivetolearn.info.

- Immordino-Yang, Mary Helen (2016). *Emotions, Learning, and the Brain.*
- Li, Jin (2003). U.S. and Chinese cultural beliefs about learning.
- Li, Jin (2004). Learning as a task or a virtue: U.S. and Chinese preschoolers explain learning.
- Li, Jin (2012). *Cultural Foundations of Learning: East and West.*
- van Egmond, Marieke, et al. (2013). Mind and virtue: The meaning of learning, a matter of culture.

Chapter Five

Discovery Step 5: Assessing Emotional Drive

Why Do East Asian Students Infuse Learning with Emotional Drive?

On a billboard in Brooklyn is the image of a handsome young man, casually dressed in white, looking self-confidently at the camera. The message? "LIVE AUTHENTICALLY."[1] What does this mean? A quick Internet search made this explanation available:[2]

> Authenticity is the development and expression of your essential self, uncensored, undiluted, unimpeded by external forces. Step one is inner authenticity: Being true to yourself, having what you think and feel follow from your beliefs, values, and purposes. Step two is outer authenticity: being true to others, having what you say and do follow from what you think and feel.

The message is this: Who you are in the world is, ideally, determined *inside yourself.*

To support that ideal, children should leave home by age 21. Teachers should "differentiate" instruction to fit each student. We all should have *thousands* of choices in our local supermarket. And each of us should pay attention to ourselves first and foremost, as suggested by the advertising slogan of a New York City pharmacy chain: "How I look. How I feel. What I need now."

"Live authentically" commands you to be internally guided, to be who you *really* are all the time. It reflects the American quest for self-expression, self-reliance, self-actualization, self-fulfillment, and self-esteem. Even if we can't do all this perfectly, it seems "natural" to us.

But for East Asians, what seems "natural" is something completely different.

SELF AND FAMILY

One thing's for sure: Each East Asian has a biological body. Within his or her body is found the same components that you and I have in ours. Each East Asian has five senses, needs to eat and sleep, inhales and exhales constantly, bleeds when cut, gradually ages, and all the rest.

Knowing this, we assume without question that individuals in Japan, China, and Korea think of *self* just like we do. They do not. If we want to understand why East Asian students infuse learning with emotional drive, then we need to begin by appreciating how they think of *self*.

What Does "Self" Mean in East Asia?

To Americans, "self" means *me*. Look up *self* in American dictionaries, and you'll find that it means "private," "personal interest," "own welfare," and an "individual's nature and character." You'll learn that each individual's self is viewed as separate from all other individuals' selves.

But those dictionaries also explain that *self* can also mean "same," "identical," and "of a single material throughout." *These* definitions move us closer to understanding East Asians.

In the United States, the quality "of a single material throughout" applies to one individual. In East Asia, it applies to a family, often to an extended family or an even larger group of relatives.

Here's another way to think about it: In the United States, "I" means *me*, and can mean nothing else but *me*, singular and unique. In Chinese, *wŏ* is the word translated as "I" in English. But *wŏ* doesn't mean *me*. To grasp what it does mean, recall the world of theater, in which actors play roles. An actor speaks of "my character," meaning the *role* that he is playing. That comes closer to the meaning of *wŏ*. It means "me *in my social role* within this group."[3]

A respected Japanese anthropologist used the example of a male Japanese child to comment on the robust concept among the Japanese of each person's roles:[4]

> The male child is trained to act or present himself in a proper way as a boy, as an elder brother, as a son and heir of a doctor, as a school child, as a first grader, as a pupil, as a neighbor, as a train passenger, and so forth. It is largely in the context of positional training that the Japanese refer to *rashii* or *rashiku*, meaning "like." The male child is told to appear or conduct himself "like a boy," "like a nursery school pupil," and so forth. The like behavior stands for a role-specific behavior bounded from the rest of the child's total existence, distinct from his nature.

An East Asian's most common role is as a member of a family (or of another very close knit group such as work peers). She views herself as whole when she's fitting into her proper place and role within her family. Since all members of a typical East Asian family feel this way, we need to think of them as *sharing a feeling of unity* that exceeds anything that we're familiar with here in the United States. Members aren't made of different stuff. They're all a "single material."

An East Asian's perspective is this: My family's welfare and interests are mine. My family's nature and character are mine. Who my family is determines how I'm known to myself and others.

Now you might be deeply dedicated to your family's welfare and interests. If you are, that gives you a head start in grasping how East Asians think of self. Your starting thought might be, "When it comes to identifying with one's family, an East Asian is just like me, *only more so*."

That's a good start . . . but it's only a start. Because if you're a typical American, you view yourself as a unique and fully independent self who has a very strong bond with your family. If you were a typical East Asian, you would not view yourself as unique or fully independent.

Figure 5.1 summarizes six revealing differences in how East Asians and Americans view themselves in relationship to their families.

Six differences in how people think of *self* and *family*	
East Asians	**Americans**
1. I am *my role* within my family.	1. I am *me*, a family member but separate.
2. Who I am is derived from my place in my family and by its standing in society.	2. Who I am is inborn and unique; I also identify with my family's other members.
3. My family's "face" or "honor" in relation to other families and society is important.	3. My personal standing in relation to my family members and others is important.
4. Family members will respect me if I read their minds and accommodate them.	4. Family members will respect me if I speak up and say what's on my mind.
5. I always support my family's interests.	5. My family should support my interests.
6. Perfecting myself through education will greatly burnish my family's "face."	6. Education, likely to improve my future, will make my parents proud of me.

Figure 5.1.

One Korean coauthor team commented on the deep contrasts in how Americans and East Asians think of themselves and in relation to others (principally, their families). They devised two simple diagrams, shown in figure 5.2, that nicely capture the difference.[5]

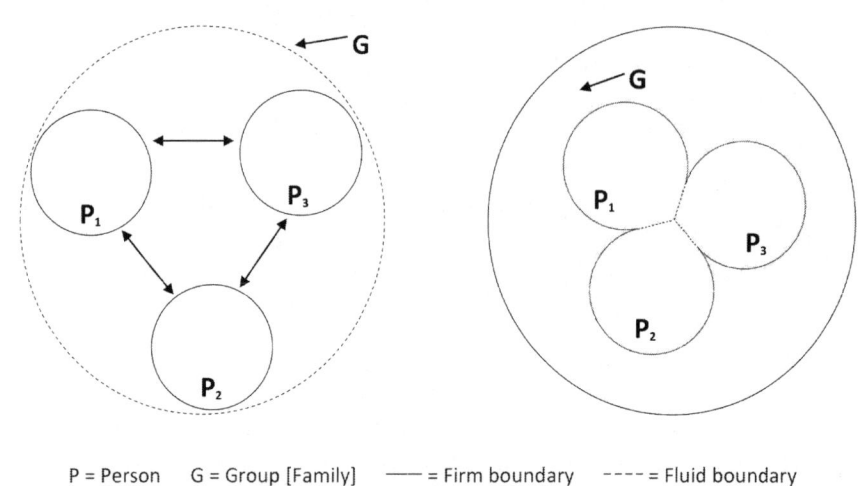

P = Person   G = Group [Family]   —— = Firm boundary   ---- = Fluid boundary

Figure 5.2. How Americans and East Asians think of themselves.
The diagram on the left represents Americans' way of thinking of themselves. Each individual is "an entity separate from every other and from the group." Individuals have "a sense of self with a sharp boundary that stops at one's skin and clearly demarks self from non-self." The diagram on the right represents East Asians' way of thinking of themselves. The group—first and foremost the family— is viewed as the unit, and as more than the mere sum of its individuals. Emphasized is the close relatedness of the individual members.
Source: Uichol Kim & Soo-Hyang Choi (1994), Individualism, collectivism, and child development: A Korean perspective. *Cross-Cultural Roots of Minority Child Development*, (Classic ed., 2014) P. M. Greenfield & R. R. Cocking, eds. Diagrams based on figures 11.1 and 11.2, pages 233 and 235.

MOTHERS AND MOTIVATION

The bonds that unite East Asian families have fascinated researchers for decades. What is their nature? How strong are they? Here are three examples of what they've learned. The first two come from studies of the drive to learn of East Asian and American students.

Motivation to Work toward Correct Answers

American educators believe that a student feels a stronger desire to work at a learning task if it's one he personally selected. Task selection by anyone else undermines his motivation. This is the big idea behind "intrinsic" motivation. Wouldn't this also be true for East Asian students?

During the 1990s, two researchers decided to find out.[6] In the San Francisco area, they studied pupils between the ages of 7 and 9. The pupils were invited to try solving anagram puzzles, in which one rearranges the letters of a word to make a new word (for instance, "silent" can be rearranged into "listen"). There were six sets of anagrams with names like Animals and Food. One group of pupils was East Asian American; the other included Americans of European descent.[7] Each group was divided into three subgroups: A, B, and C.

A. Personal choice: Each pupil freely selected which set of anagrams she would try.
B. Stranger's choice: The researcher told each pupil which set of anagrams to try.
C. Mother's choice: Each pupil was given a set of anagrams and told that her mother had selected it.

One would expect that, if American ideas about intrinsic motivation applied worldwide, all of the pupils in subgroup A would show the greatest motivation to try solving the anagrams.

One way to gauge each pupil's motivation is to see how many anagrams he or she completes correctly. Each pupil was given six minutes. Figure 5.3 illustrates the outcomes.[8]

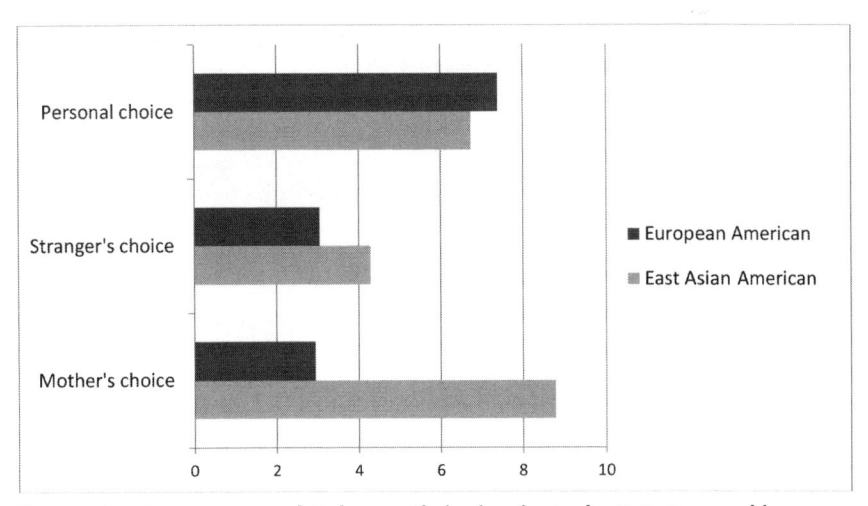

Figure 5.3. Anagrams completed correctly in six minutes by 7- to 9-year-olds.
Source: Sheena Iyengar & Mark Lepper (1999), Rethinking the value of choice: A cultural perspective on intrinsic motivation. *Journal of Personality and Social Psychology*, 76(3). This graph closely reproduces figure 1, page 353.

40 Chapter Five

The American 7- to 9-year-olds confirmed our educators' belief about intrinsic motivation. They correctly completed more than twice as many anagrams when *they* chose which set to work on, compared with both Stranger's Choice and Mother's Choice. Notice on figure 5.3 that there is virtually no difference between Stranger's Choice and Mother's Choice.

The East Asian American children did something different. When they personally chose which set to work on, they completed more anagrams than when a stranger chose for them. But look at their Mother's Choice performance: it's the highest number of completions in figure 5.3!

Motivation to Work Instead of Play

The researchers ran a second experiment. This time they wanted to see what each child did during a six-minute "free play" period. This experiment began as soon as the first one (above) was finished. The researcher said to the child, "I must go to score your work. I'll be gone for several minutes." What the researcher said next differed for subgroups A, B, and C:[9]

A. Personal choice: "So do whatever you want for a while. There's more anagrams, there's some crossword puzzles over there . . . whatever you like."
B. Stranger's choice: "While I'm out, I want you to work on *this* set of anagrams [gives the child one set]. There are six colored markers for jotting down your answers. I want you to use *this* one [gives the child one marker]."
C. Mother's choice: "While I'm out, please work on more anagrams. When your mother filled out your consent form, she decided which set of anagrams she wants you to do. Let me see . . . [he flips through a stack of consent forms]. OK, it's *this* set [gives the child one set]. Oh, your mom also said which color marker you should use. It's *this* one [gives the child one marker]."

You need to know that, within the room during all experiments, there were *three* people: the child, the researcher, and an observer. After the researcher departed, the observer faked a big yawn and said to the child, "I'm really busy right now, so just do whatever you wish." He then hunched over his books and papers as though he were studying. But he wasn't. Concealed under the books and papers he had a stopwatch. He recorded how long the child worked on anagrams out of a total of 360 seconds. Figure 5.4 summarizes what the children did.[10]

Again, the American 7- to 9-year-olds confirmed American educators' belief about intrinsic motivation. They spent more than triple the amount of

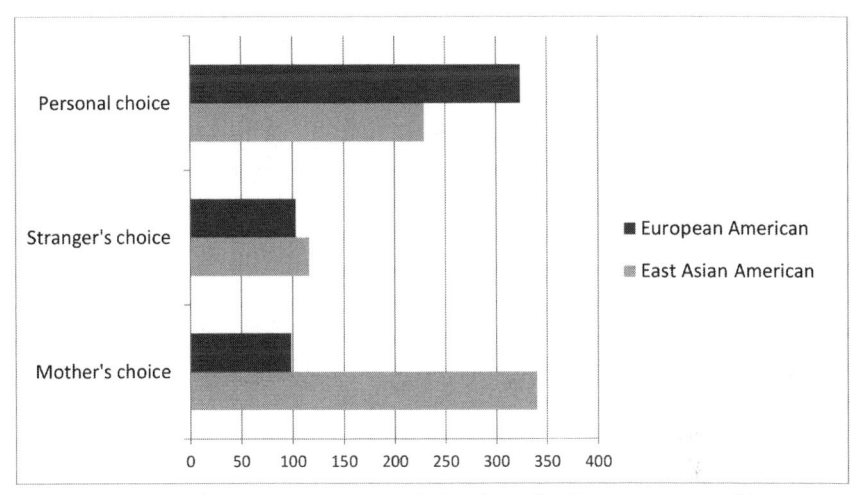

Figure 5.4. Seconds spent on anagrams during free play by 7- to 9-year-olds.
Source: Sheena Iyengar & Mark Lepper (1999), Rethinking the value of choice: A cultural perspective on intrinsic motivation. *Journal of Personality and Social Psychology*, 76(3). This graph closely reproduces figure 2, page 354.

time on anagrams when *they* chose what to do, compared with both Stranger's Choice and Mother's Choice. Once again there's almost no difference between Stranger's Choice and Mother's Choice.

Again, the East Asian American children did something different. Look at their Mother's Choice performance: They logged the most seconds—340 out of 360—in figure 5.4.

This two-part study was one of the first to reveal the deep bonds within East Asian families, in this case between mothers and their children. If a child performs best when her *mother* chooses the task, then the child must have a powerful sense of unity with her mother. The child's feeling of unity would be blended with feelings of respect and loyalty toward her mother.[11] And the child's performances on the mother-chosen tasks were the *most outstanding* performances of all.

If you were one of the researchers who discovered this, wouldn't you question whether our American beliefs about "intrinsic motivation" are true of human beings everywhere?

Searching for "Self" inside the Brain

About the same time that this study was completed, machines for peering inside brains became available. One, called a "functional magnetic resonance imaging" device, or fMRI, measures neurological activity in specific brain areas by detecting changes in blood flow.[12] That's because when any area of the brain becomes active, blood flow there increases.

Neurologists had long known that an area in the brain behind one's forehead, the "medial prefrontal cortex," or mPFC, is strongly involved in many higher cognitive functions. Most important for us is that the mPFC is the home of memory and behavior related to self. Your mPFC is where you have thoughts, emotions, and memories, and make plans, related to yourself.

Because the level of neurological activity in the mPFC can be measured, we should be able to discover, for various individuals, *who is included in "self."*

This is exactly what four Chinese researchers decided to do in the early 2000s.[13] Using an fMRI device, they peered into the brains of 13 Western college students in Beijing who had been studying there for under a year, and of 13 Chinese college students. (The Westerners were from Britain, the United States, Australia, and Canada.)

Each student was asked to judge whether a series of words was proper to describe himself, his mother, and "other." (For the Westerners, "other" was Bill Clinton; for the Chinese it was Zhu Rongji, a former premier of China). Hundreds of descriptive adjectives such as "brave" and "childish" were tested, using English for the Westerners and Chinese characters for the Chinese.

Here's how each test proceeded: The student was asked, "Does this adjective describe you?" or ". . . your mother?" or ". . . Bill Clinton?" At once, a word such as "brave" would appear on a monitor and the student would respond yes or no. Simultaneously, the fMRI device was busily scanning to determine whether activity in that student's mPFC was changing, and by how much.

When the students were asked to make judgments about themselves, both Westerners and Chinese showed an increase in mPFC activity, with the Chinese mPFCs showing slightly more.

When the students were asked to make a judgment about "other" (Bill Clinton or Zhu Rongji), both Westerners and Chinese showed a decrease in mPFC activity, with the Westerners showing a much larger decrease.

But when the students were asked to make a judgment about their mother, the Westerners showed a *decrease* in mPFC activity, while the Chinese showed an *increase* in mPFC activity.

These findings are portrayed in figure 5.5.[14]

The Chinese students, when thinking of their mother *and* their self, showed an *increase* in mPFC activity—with the increase in the case of their mothers being much greater. But for the Westerners, the mPFC showed increased activity *only* when they thought of their self.

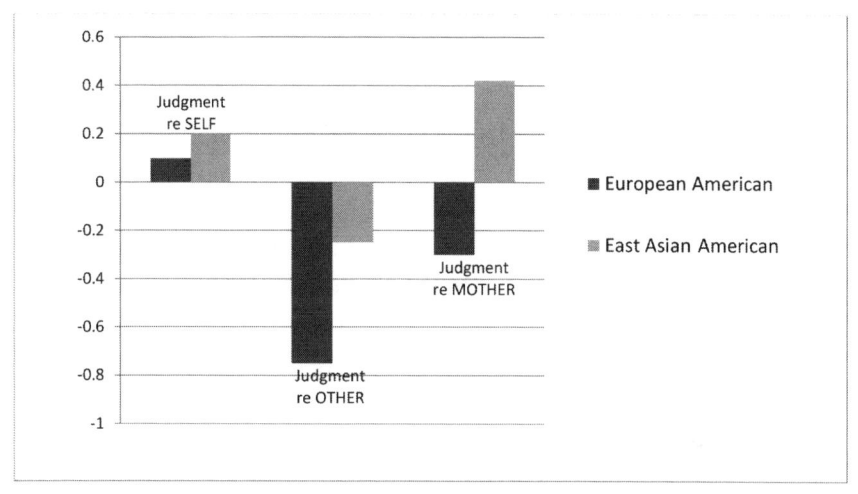

Figure 5.5. Percentage change in fMRI signal from median prefrontal cortex.
Source: Ying Zhu et al. (2007), Neural basis of cultural influence on self-representation. Neurolmage, 34 (3). This graph closely reproduces figure 4c, page 1315, which is discussed on pages 1312–1313. Precise percentage figures are not provided by Zhu et al. in either the text or the figure.

The Western students, when thinking of both their mothers and a public figure not personally known to them, showed a *decrease* in mPFC activity. This finding strongly suggests that, for Westerners, mother and "other" are in a similar mental category.

This neuroimaging study, and several others similar to it,[15] demonstrate that "self" in East Asia means something significantly more inclusive, and less separated, than it means to us.

SELF, EMOTION, AND THE DRIVE TO LEARN

From infancy, an East Asian learns to consider herself as whole when fitting into her proper place and role within her extended family. She recognizes but doesn't emphasize her differences from family members. She focuses instead on her togetherness and unity with them. She is necessary to them. She learns to fill and amplify her role among them. She thinks of "self" as *us*, not as *me*.

In her 2016 book, *Grit*, psychologist Angela Duckworth clarifies the meaning of "purpose" as "the idea that what we do matters to people other than ourselves." Her research has identified *other-directed purpose* as one of the key wellsprings of passion and perseverance.[16]

Sebastian Junger's 2016 book, *Tribe*, captures the profound sense of commonality felt by people who actively pursue a cause that gives their lives a *strongly shared purpose*. They devote "their energies toward the good of the community rather than just themselves."[17]

Why do East Asian students infuse learning with fervent emotional drive? Because acting for the benefit of one's whole family is much more strongly motivating than acting for the benefit of one's separated self. Within the family is where one's most enduring relationships thrive. Family gives identity and significance to one's life, positive emotions that one wants to protect and promote. *What's in it for me?* is about a benefit for one. *What's in it for us?* is about a benefit for those with whom one shares ancestors and aspirations, a benefit for one's *whole "self."*

Learning in school—learning to the point of mastery—is an earnestly desired goal of the East Asian "self." Dr. Jin Li, whom we met in Discovery Step 4, gave it a name: *hào xúe xīn*, "Heart and mind for wanting to learn,"[18] but in this book we're calling it "the drive to learn."

Where did this fervent drive come from?

HOW STEP 5 ADVANCED OUR DISCOVERY PROCESS

We began by needing to know *why* East Asian students infuse learning with emotional drive. So we probed the meaning of "self" in the United States and East Asia. Here is what we learned:

- In the United States, "self" refers to the individual not only physically but in every other way. Who one is, what one does—and why—all should be determined *internally* by that individual.
- In East Asia, "self" doesn't refer to one individual, but to her *together with*, and *in unity with*, the family in which she was raised. Research shows that "me" and "mother" are virtually indistinguishable in East Asians' minds. In fact, research suggests that "mother" can be more influential than "me" in their minds.
- The reason why East Asian students infuse learning with fervent emotional drive, then, is because their families infuse learning with emotional drive. It's important to note that this is identical to saying that East Asian students *internally* infuse learning with emotional drive.

The linkage of family, learning, and virtue is an enduring cultural trait of East Asians, one that developed over millennia. We need to discover more about its origin and nature. To do that well, we need to think in new ways: first like a sociologist (step 6), then like a historian (step 7).

FURTHER READING

If you'd like more detail about the researchers' findings, or simply wish to know what inspired the contents of Discovery Step 5, read the following entries in the annotated bibliography at www.thedrivetolearn.info.

- Bao, Xue-hua, & Shui-fong Lam (2008). Who makes the choice? Rethinking the role of autonomy and relatedness in Chinese children's motivation.
- Biggs, John B. (1996a). Learning, schooling, and socialization: A Chinese solution to a Western problem.
- Cheng, Rebecca Wing-yi, et al. (2016). Motivation of Chinese learners: An integration of etic and emic approaches.
- Fogel, Alan, et al. (1992). A comparison of the parent-child relationship in Japan and the United States.
- Fong, Ricci W., & Man Tak Yuen (2016). The role of self-efficacy and connectedness in the academic success of Chinese learners.
- Fu, Alyssa S., & Hazel Rose Markus (2014). My mother and me: Why tiger mothers motivate Asian Americans but not European Americans.
- Hsu, Francis L. K. (1981). *Americans & Chinese: Passage to Differences* (3rd ed.). [See the chapter titled "The Beginnings of Contrast."]
- Iyengar, Sheena, & Mark Lepper (1999). Rethinking the value of choice: A cultural perspective on intrinsic motivation.
- Kim, Uichol, & Soo-Hyang Choi (1994). Individualism, collectivism, and child development: A Korean perspective.
- Lebra, Takie Sugiyama (1994). Mother and child in Japanese socialization: A Japan-U.S. comparison.
- Markus, Hazel Rose, & Shinobu Kitayama (1991). Culture and the self: Implications for cognition, emotion, and motivation.
- Park, Young-Shin, & Uichol Kim (2006). Family, parent-child relationship, and academic achievement in Korea: Indigenous cultural and psychological analysis.
- Pratt, Daniel D. (1991). Conceptions of self within China and the United States: Contrasting foundations for adult education.
- Zhu, Ying, et al. (2007). Neural basis of cultural influence on self-representation.

Chapter Six

Discovery Step 6: Thinking like a Sociologist

Do Sociological Factors Help Explain East Asians' Fervent Drive to Learn?

In his 1989 book, *To Open Minds*, the eminent psychologist and educator Howard Gardner shares his experiences during four trips to China to study early childhood education there. On one occasion, he, his wife, and their year-and-a-half-old son, Benjamin, were staying at a hotel in Nanjing. Their room key was attached to a large plastic block, intended to discourage a guest from leaving the hotel without turning in the key. It could be handed to the desk attendant or dropped through a slot. The slot was narrow, requiring that the pendant be aligned just so.

Benjamin liked to drop the key through the slot, but rarely could. He loved to bang the key all around the slot, enjoying the noise it made. Here's Gardner continuing the story:[1]

> Any Chinese attendant nearby—and sometimes even a mere Chinese passerby—would come over to watch Benjamin. As soon as the observer saw . . . [Benjamin's] lack of initial success at the appointed task, she (or, less often, he) attempted to intervene. In general, she would hold onto his hand and, gently but firmly, guide it directly toward the slot, reorient it as necessary, and help Benjamin insert the key. She would then smile somewhat expectantly at Ellen or me, as if awaiting a thank you—and on occasion would frown slightly, as if to admonish the negligent parent.
>
> [During our four visits to China, adults would frequently approach Benjamin, often to assist him] with some task—retrieving a ball with which he was playing, helping him to sit straight in his seat, fixing his shirttail or his shoes, directing him away from a perilous ledge, or guiding the stroller he was awkwardly pushing around.

What's going on here? By the end of this Discovery Step, we'll understand.

Chapter Six

LEARNING IN DIFFERENT SOCIETIES

Think about this: All the stuff you deal with every day—people, places, situations, decisions, plans, problems, finances, computers, and such—is incredibly complex as well as hugely diverse.

Scientists tell us that *nothing even comes close* to the human brain's capacity for handling information, maintaining relationships, solving problems, devising new ideas, and all the other tasks it does for us. On the day you were born, was your brain able to accomplish all that? No.

Was it able to learn *how to accomplish* each of those tasks? Well . . . sort of . . .

Was it able to learn *how to learn*? Yes. Our foundational skill is how to identify, acquire, retain, and apply the skills and information we need to survive and thrive. *How* we learn is basic.

It's no surprise that *what* an infant learns depends on where it lives. Is it freezing all the time, or hot and humid? What must be learned will differ. Do adults rely on labor-saving machines made by others, or on their own wits, cooperation, and toil? What must be learned will differ.

But here's the thing: where an infant lives also directly impacts *how* he learns to learn.

The *what* and the *how* of learning equally depend on the *where*. So let's put on our sociologist hat, jump back into our helicopter, and look down again at broad categories of human experience.

Two Broad Types of Societies

Every society, today and in the past, has unique qualities. Nonetheless, sociologists have lumped them together into a variety of broad types. Two of those types are useful for us now:[2]

- **Individualized societies:** This is the type with which we are familiar. Other names for this type include urban, technological, industrialized, knowledge, and Western.[3] Beginning with the Renaissance, and building on the intellectual legacy of ancient Greece (discussed in the next Discovery Step), these societies became increasingly more complex. To thrive within them, individuals needed to acquire ever more specialized skills and knowledge. Schools came into being, in part, to teach the various specializations to the next generation.

    From a sociological perspective, a hallmark of these societies came to be the assumption that a child would become ever more independent minded as he grows up, eventually leaving his family of birth and—relying on specialized skills and knowledge—make his own way in the world. Another hallmark is the characteristic ways in which parents raise their children, expecting that they would *and should* gradually become self-reliant in thought and deed.

- **Communitarian societies:** This type remained subsistence-based longer than the societies that became individualized; a few remain subsistence-based to this day. Through hunting-gathering and small-scale agriculture, families obtained food, clothing, and shelter for their own needs, with little left for trade. To survive, people had to be directly engaged with their environment, adapting to its changing impact on their subsistence activities.

From a sociological perspective, a hallmark of communitarian societies is the assumption that children would remain in or near their birth communities, or at least would maintain tight social and emotional ties with their families. Another hallmark is the characteristic ways in which parents raise their children. They expect children to fit into the family's patterns of daily interaction and to contribute to its welfare. They also expect children to see themselves, and to be seen by others, as wholly identified with the family unit, not as separate and unique.

These patterns of human relationships explain why sociologists categorize East Asian societies as communitarian. Actually, most of these societies today are global leaders in the development and application of technology, and they have long had schools and universities.

These two types of society are a study in contrasts. Adults need to build relationships and behave socially in contrasting ways. To ensure that their infants gain social competence, parents not only teach them different things—the *what*—they also use different approaches and have different expectations about the ways in which their infant should go about learning—the *how*.

What, exactly, do the parents do? Around 2000, a German researcher studied how parents raise very young children in two representative societies. For a modernized, individual-focused society, she chose her own: urban middle-class Germany. For a subsistence-based, community-oriented society, she chose that of the Nso people, a group of farmers in rural Cameroon.

Learning to Thrive in an Individualized Society[4]

In Germany, eye contact and talk were key modes of mother-infant communication. A mother often brought her infant's face inches from her own, often by lifting him to the eye-to-eye position. The infant could gaze into his mother's eyes, or close his eyes or look away. Mothers liked their infant's gaze—and were disappointed when he looked away. They often "talked" with their infant, taking turns despite his babbling sounds. They also stimulated him with toys and other items. They were eager for smiling and happy sounds, which they saw as evidence of emerging uniqueness and independence. If happy signs were absent, the infant was coaxed: "Give Mommy a smile."

A goal of the parents was to ensure that their infant learned to accept temporary separation from them. He wasn't constantly held, nor was he always near to an adult caretaker; he was expected to spend time alone. He rarely slept with an adult; he had his own bed. Parents didn't respond instantly to every sign that their baby wanted something or was in distress.

Parents assumed that natural maturation was the principal driver of their child's physical and mental development. They were eager to see evidence of growth. For example, they were happy when the child took initiative in learning by means of trial and error, discovery, or asking good questions. They applauded signs that their child was gaining new abilities, especially increases in rational thinking and practical know-how about his human and physical surroundings.[5]

Learning to Thrive in a Communitarian Society[6]

The child-rearing study in Cameroon revealed many contrasting patterns. Very important for Nso mothers was physical closeness and emotional warmth with their infants. The two were in constant contact, skin-to-skin; the Nso have a word for this, *koyti*, meaning feeling good through body contact. Breastfeeding occurred often. The mother *anticipated her infant's desire* to suckle and instantly offered her breast (seemingly quicker than "on demand"). Infants never slept alone.

The researcher showed the Nso mothers videotapes she had made of German women and their infants. When the Nso saw that German mothers weren't almost always skin-to-skin with their infants, one cried, "Those mothers handle the children as if they were not *their* babies!"

The Nso didn't assume that infants develop mainly through natural maturation. They believed that parents must actively guide and train their child. Parents cared greatly about motor (physical) development, which would enable the child to contribute to the family's subsistence activities. To this end, mothers routinely stimulated their infant's body according to local custom.[7]

Parents also cared greatly about their child's development of *social* competence: how to fit into an interdependent community where cooperation and hierarchy are valued. The child gained social skills by participation, imitation, and directive guidance by others with more experience. Her guides and mentors for fitting in were her older siblings at least as often as her parents.

Figure 6.1 summarizes what was discovered about both Cameroonian and German parenting.

Two models of infancy and parenting of small children	
Model in Communitarian Societies represented by Nso farmers of Cameroon	**Model in Individualized Societies** represented by urban middle-class Germans
Young Nso children were…	Young German children were…
1. maintained in constant bodily contact with their mothers, fostering feelings of interdependence.	1. encouraged to develop awareness of their separateness and independence as early as possible.
2. conditioned by experiences to expect cooperative human relations through empathetic responses to others' needs.	2. given opportunities to realize that they can, and should, have some control in their interactions with everyone else.
3. expected to develop as an outcome of guidance and training provided by their parents and older siblings.	3. expected to develop naturally, and on that basis to increasingly take initiative for their own learning and skill-building.
4. applauded both for *physical* gains and increased *social* ability to contribute to, and fit into, their family and community.	4. applauded for *mental* gains such as increased rational thinking and practical know-how about their surroundings.
5. dealt with as novices or apprentices in need of guidance and instruction by more competent experts and seniors.	5. dealt with increasingly as the social and intellectual equals of other individuals, including their parents.
6. assumed to be growing into adults who would remain physically, or at least socially and emotionally, united with their birth family.	6. assumed to be growing into adults who would physically and socially leave the family to make their way in the world.

Figure 6.1.

Insights from another Communitarian Society[8]

Another useful study compared 5- to 11-year-old children in a communitarian society, that of the Mayans of Guatemala, with children of middle-class Americans of European background. The researchers wanted to discover how attentive these older children were to instruction that was not intended for them. So they devised a situation in which one child was shown how to assemble a toy frog while his or her older sibling was seated a short distance away with a "distracter toy."

About ten days later, both siblings were brought back to the facility. The older sibling, who had observed from a distance, was given an opportunity to assemble the frog. Both sessions were videotaped. Here's what the videotapes revealed about the 20 sibling pairs from each society:

- During session 1, the older Mayan siblings engaged in more sustained attention to the nearby instruction than the older American siblings. The older American siblings usually paid no attention at all or gave only brief glances.[9]
- During session 2, the older Mayan siblings were more adept in assembling the frog than the older Americans. Statistical procedures confirmed that prior sustained attention was a significant factor in enabling the older siblings to assemble the frog.[10]

The researchers cited many preceding studies in North and Central American indigenous communities that yielded similar findings. All of that research, they wrote,[11]

> noted children's keen observation of the activities in their community, as they were integrated in everyday work and social life. Learning by attending to ongoing events and beginning to pitch in when ready seem to be key features of a cultural pattern . . . , forming a system dubbed *intent community participation*.
> Similarly, Navajo children are incorporated "in every life task, so that children learn themselves, by keen observation. Mothers do not teach their daughters to weave, but one day a girl may say, 'I am ready. Let me weave.'"
> Learning by intent community participation would necessarily be more limited in European American middle-class communities, where children are routinely segregated from community work and many social activities. For example, . . . children are rarely present, and may not be allowed, in workplaces as adults go about earning their livelihood.

Children in communitarian societies learn to be attentive to a wide range of activities occurring around them. Except in schools (to the extent that the society has schools), most of those activities are *not for or about children*. After weaning (relatively late), children usually spend much of their time in the company of other children; adults rarely try to manage or direct them. Yet the vast majority of the children learn to be competent in their societies, and to thrive as adults. *They do this by learning to be quietly receptive to all sorts of learning opportunities.*

LEARNING TO BE COMPETENT; LEARNING IN SCHOOL

These overviews give us a window into the *cultures of learning* typical of individualized and communitarian societies around the world. A culture of learning means that, within a society, there are certain ways and means for teaching and learning that most people agree on and usually apply.

This brings us to an especially important point: A culture of learning isn't only about how parents, siblings, and other caretakers think and behave as they prepare a child for life in their society. *A culture of learning is also about how the child himself learns how to learn.* It's about what the child comes to expect of others, and of himself, within any situation that has an opportunity to learn knowledge or skills.

That includes learning in school.

Some communitarian societies have no schools. Others have long had them. Others gained schools during modernization. Imagine an infant growing up in a society with communitarian patterns of child-rearing *and* schools that the child will begin to attend at age 5 or 6.

Our infant is gradually gaining self-awareness and consciousness of her surroundings. Her brain's synapses are forming their first, deepest connections. Her consistent experience is that her parents, older siblings, and other caretakers are close and warm with her, feel empathy for others, uphold cooperation within the group, and defer to more experienced seniors. Older kinfolk are caringly directing her learning—how to walk, put on clothes, show respect, weed the garden, fetch firewood. Eventually she realizes that she fits in best by being receptive to them.

Why do her older kinfolk *caringly* direct her learning? Because they have a stake in the outcome. She isn't just an adorable cherub who tugs at their heartstrings. She is *One of Them*. Furthermore, she has economic value! She has one more mouth to feed, so she must pull her weight. She must contribute to essential subsistence activities and, soon, help to raise her yet-to-be-born siblings. Family members need her to fit in cooperatively, competently, and smoothly, and to carry out ever more demanding survival-relevant roles.

When it's time for her to learn reading, writing, and arithmetic, *how will she do that?*

Learning How to Learn in East Asian Schools

The studies in Cameroon and Guatemala are merely two of many studies of child-rearing in communitarian societies.[12] Such societies have local and regional differences, of course. Yet virtually all studies in communitarian societies reveal that adults share similar meanings of competence, and similar approaches to ensure that children become competent. Summing up all the findings from many communitarian societies, the German researcher offered observations that support this book's theme:[13]

The hierarchical structure and the teaching mode of the early interactions prepare the infant to be unanimously attentive to the caregiving environment. This attention is mainly expressed *by attentive listening and observation.*

In Discovery Step 7, in which we'll think like a historian, we'll find that China is known to have relied on small-scale, village-based agriculture beginning some 5,000 years ago. All three East Asian societies have long demonstrated the child-rearing patterns of communitarian societies.

In one way, however, ancient China departed from the communitarian pattern: While millions of subsistence farmers were toiling in the fields, a few scholars began writing poetry and prose that eventually became "the classics." Several thousand years later, the Imperial Examination system raised the classics to prominence. Those exams gave *anyone*, even a poor farmer's son, hope that he could vault from daily toil into wealth, power, and everyone's respect. IF . . .

IF he mastered—*mastered!*—the classics.

How did a poor farmer's son expect to do that?

Today it's an East Asian girl arriving at the schoolhouse door to learn reading, writing, and arithmetic. A thousand years ago it was her ancestor, the farmer's son, intending to gain power and prestige by mastering classic literature. What do these two young people have in common?

Before they hit the books, they already know how to learn. They know how to be diligently receptive to others who care about them and have already mastered whatever is to be learned.

THE EPISODE WITH THE KEY

In his book, *Open Minds*, Howard Gardner (1989) has a great deal to say about the episode of Benjamin with the key. Everywhere he went in China, he was asked to give talks to Chinese educators. He decided to begin telling the key story, and to seek the reactions of audience members:[14]

> [Almost all said that] since adults *know* how to place the key in the key slot . . . , since that is the ultimate purpose of approaching the slot . . . , what possible gain is achieved by having the child flail about? . . . Why not show him what to do? He will be happy . . . , he will learn how to accomplish the task sooner, and then he can proceed to more complex activities, like opening the door or asking for the key—both of which accomplishments can (and should) in due course be modeled for him as well.

Here's the answer to my "What's going on here?" question. Benjamin's American parents assumed that natural maturation was the principal driver of his physical and mental development. They were happy when Benjamin took initiative in learning by means of trial and error, discovery, and such, which is precisely how they interpreted his flailing away at the key slot. Eventually, through a mix of (a) naturally occurring maturation and (b) self-initiated trial-and-error discovery learning, Benjamin would figure out *on his own* how to smoothly insert the key. His eventual success would bring applause from his American parents because . . .[15]

> We were trying to teach Benjamin something: that one can solve a problem effectively by oneself. Such self-reliance is a principal value of child rearing in middle-class America. [But if] the child is shown exactly how to do something—whether it be placing a key in the key slot, drawing a rooster, or making amends for a misdeed—he is less likely to figure out himself how to accomplish such a task.

But Benjamin's faltering efforts occurred in China, where the culture of learning is different. The Chinese did not assume that natural maturation was the principal driver of child development. But they did care about child development, wanted it to proceed apace, and took direct measures to that end. They guided Benjamin's learning, but not via talk or encouragement. *They grasped Benjamin's hand and physically showed him, modeled for him, the moves to smoothly insert the key into the slot.* They interactively participated with Benjamin in order to guide his learning. They assumed that Benjamin would appreciate their hands-on, you-do-it-*this*-way instruction.

HOW STEP 6 ADVANCED OUR DISCOVERY PROCESS

We began by asking whether sociological factors help explain East Asians' fervent drive to learn. We learned about *cultures of learning*, which greatly advances our discovery process:

- *Culture of learning* refers to how a society's adults ensure that their children learn the right things. It *also* refers to what the child comes to expect of others, *and of himself*, within any situation in which he's learning knowledge or skills. It's about how he learns how to learn.
- In individualized societies, cultures of learning emphasize a child's mental development via independent exploration and natural maturation. Parents manage their child's time and try to focus his attention in ways they think will support exploration and maturation. They rarely instruct their child directly because they see this as undermining his self-reliant exploration.

- In communitarian societies, cultures of learning emphasize a child's physical and social development via direct instruction by expert others, initially the parents and later the older siblings and others. Occasions for direct instruction occur spontaneously during every day; but except for schooling, rarely are attempts made to manage a child's time or attention.
- In communitarian societies (where children's time is not managed), children pay attention to, and learn from, a wide range of activities that happen to be occurring in their vicinity.
- By the time a child raised in a communitarian society goes to school, she knows *how to be diligently receptive to others who have already mastered whatever is to be learned.*
- Despite extensive modernization, the societies of East Asia have deep historical roots in ways of social and family life that give them many characteristics of communitarian societies.

In Discovery Step 5, we found that East Asians' emotional drive to learn comes from their linking of learning with family and virtue. That linkage developed over millennia; we realized that we need to know more about it. To do that well, we first needed to think like a sociologist, which we've just done. Now we need to think like a historian, which is our next step—step 7.

FURTHER READING

If you'd like more detail about the researchers' findings, or simply wish to know what inspired the contents of Discovery Step 6, read the following entries in the annotated bibliography at www.thedrivetolearn.info.

- Boe, Erling E., Henry May, & Robert F. Boruch (2002). Student task persistence in the Third International Mathematics and Science Study: A major source of achievement differences . . .
- Chao, Ruth K., & Vivian Tseng (2002). Parenting in Asia.
- Gardner, Howard (1989). *To Open Minds: Chinese Clues to the Dilemma of Contemporary Education.*
- Grove, Cornelius (2006). Understanding the two instructional style prototypes.
- Keller, Heidi (2003). Socialization for competence: Cultural models of infancy.
- Kim, Uichol, & Soo-Hyang Choi (1994). Individualism, collectivism, and child development: A Korean perspective.

- Park, Young-Shin, & Uichol Kim (2006). Family, parent-child relationship, and academic achievement in Korea.
- Peak, Lois (1991). Training learning skills and attitudes in Japanese early education settings.
- Shimahara, Nobuo K., & Akira Sakai (1995). *Learning to Teach in Two Cultures: Japan and the United States.*

Chapter Seven

Discovery Step 7: Thinking like a Historian

Do Historical Factors Help Explain East Asians' Fervent Drive to Learn?

David Lancy probably knows more about *what*, *why*, and *how* children learn than anyone else on the planet. Lancy collects and studies the works of anthropologists and historians who, since the early 20th century, have explored how children are raised in societies worldwide. His most recent book, *The Anthropology of Childhood,* 2nd ed. (2015), includes a "Society Index" listing over 450 societies—not only China, Japan, Korea, and the United States, but also Pirahã, Qashqa'i, Baulè, !Kung, and others you probably have never even heard of—where researchers have studied children.

So if you're craving a grand overview of how children learn to become contributing members of their societies, no one is better prepared to look down from that imaginary helicopter and see the broadest of Big Pictures. From that lofty vantage point, here's what Lancy reports:[1]

> Children across cultures and through time have managed to grow to adulthood and learn to become functioning members of society without the necessity of schooling.

Children do not need schools: That's Lancy's first Big Picture conclusion. His second is that classroom instruction for children arose due to the growing complexity of societies (which required learned administrators) and the increasing specialization of craftsmen.

Lancy's final Big Picture conclusion is that children resist schooling because it requires them to curb their exuberance, sit still, and focus attention. Everywhere schools have come into being, students are reluctant to behave in a way that makes group learning possible. They must be "tamed." In some cases, says Lancy, their resistance is *overcome*; in others, it's *prevented*.

TAMING STUDENTS IN AMERICA

If we dig deeply into history, we find that the earliest story of student resistance to group learning comes from a Bronze Age classroom, where students learned to write on clay tablets. One student wrote, "My headmaster read my tablet, said, 'There is something missing,' caned me. 'Why didn't you speak Sumerian,' caned me. And so I began to hate the scribal art."[2]

Throughout Western history, a teacher's badge of authority was an object used to inflict pain. In Greece, it was the *narthex*, a stalk of giant fennel. In Rome, it was a whip. In Renaissance Italy, it was a rod. In Britain, it was a "birch" (a bundle of twigs). Says Lancy, "These practices grew out of the belief that children would not naturally accept the role of student."[3]

In the New England colonies before the American Revolution, the beliefs of John Calvin prevailed: Newborns shared the Original Sin of Adam and Eve and were "by nature, depraved." Their parents had to quickly guarantee that the child would live a godly life, and therefore were expected to "break the will" of their tiny child through harsh discipline, training, and church-going. All of this occurred before the child's schooling—similarly harsh—began.[4]

Why are children in the West so determined to do what *they* want to do? The physiological energy of childhood is part of the explanation. But there's also a cultural part. It takes us back to ancient Greece, which historians say was the place where basic Western values were born.

Ways of Life in Ancient Greece

Greece is a land of mountains, rivers, and valleys. In ancient times, these landforms led to two outcomes. First, agriculture on a large scale was impossible; most people lived by herding and fishing. Second, people organized themselves into hundreds of small city-states, which retained their independence from each other.

Within the city-states, it was rare for a powerful ruler to emerge. Far more common were arrangements whereby public decisions were made by groups, including—most famously in Athens—by almost all of a city's citizens meeting in assembly. In fact, "democracy" comes from the Greek word *dēmokratia*, meaning "the people" and "rule, power."

One factor making democracy possible in ancient Greece was that a tradition of discussion and debate had arisen. Individuals were expected to make up their own minds and to exchange their opinions with each other. (Think of Socrates, who engaged his students in dialogues.) Contributing to this tradition of openness to fresh ideas is that Greece was a crossroads of trade, which continually introduced new ideas to the public.

Greek Ways of Life Continue Today

We think of ancient Greece as "the cradle of democracy." It's also *the cradle of individualism*. A Greek lived in a culture where he could pretty much decide for himself what to think and do. His opinions counted. He could befriend people outside his family. He could convince others of his ideas . . . or at least try. He felt relatively little pressure to conform to the expectations of others.

The individual-focused values of ancient Greece played a key role in forming today's Western values and mindsets. Even the ways in which Western people *think* can be traced to Greece.[5] In the United States during the 19th century, individual-focused values were strengthened by the experience of frontiersmen and wilderness settlers. These ways of life are what American parents transmit to their children . . . by precept *and* by example.

So it's not surprising that American children bring into classrooms an expectation that what *they* want to do will be taken into account. At home, each has been learning a critical message: Who you are in the world, and what you do, should be determined *inside yourself*. (Even children who eat in high chairs are asked if they prefer Raisin Bran or Cheerios for breakfast!) This is a key reason why, as Lancy says, children must be "tamed" if learning in classrooms is to occur.

Across more than 2,000 years of history, Western students' resistance to classroom learning was tamed almost entirely by the proverbial "stick." In American schools right up through the early 20th century, punishments were generously applied by teachers in order to tame students.

The Carrot Replaces the Stick

There was a contrary opinion: The "carrot" would work better than the stick. The first person to express this view was the Roman philosopher Quintilian, born in Iberia about the time Jesus was crucified (35 AD). He said that "learning through play" was preferable for young children.[6]

In 1693, the English philosopher John Locke published *Some Thoughts Concerning Education*, in which he strongly disapproved of any kind of corporal punishment or "breaking the will." He called instead for kindness simply because it's effective. In 1762, Jean-Jacques Rousseau, the French philosopher, published *Émile; or, On Education*. He advocated that young children not be sent to school at all, but given an opportunity to grow according to their natural tendencies.[7]

In the United States during the 1800s, authors and speakers began to push back against Calvin's "break the will" ideas, proposing gentle methods of child-rearing and teaching. They said that newborn infants are morally Good and capable of a glorious unfolding, like that of a flower. Their view also included the belief that children are mentally fragile and easily exhausted. These ideas slowly gained acceptance, in part because a theme of the 19th century's popular romantic poets was children's moral goodness, glorious unfolding, and delicate mental capacity.[8]

During the 20th century, beliefs shifted from emphasizing sticks to emphasizing carrots. Not everyone became a believer, but most authorities did. They said the way to overcome children's resistance to classroom learning was *to motivate them to want* to curb their exuberance and focus attention. In short: "What *we* have for you to do is more interesting than what *you* want to do!"

Regardless of whether American adults use sticks or carrots, children's resistance is being *overcome*. David Lancy tells us of another way: children's resistance can be *prevented*.

TAMING STUDENTS IN EAST ASIA

Children's resistance to classroom learning is largely *prevented* in East Asia. To understand how this came about, we need to consider the ancient history of China.

Ways of Life in Ancient China

First of all, the geography of China was different from that of Greece. There were mountains, but in between them were vast stretches of flat, fertile land that invited agriculture. Archaeological evidence reveals that crops were being routinely grown in China around 5000 BCE. Agriculture required the inhabitants of small rural villages to work together toward a common goal. That, in turn, required organization, planning, and coordination: in short, leadership.

Society in ancient China was organized around villages and family clans. "Village" and "clan" often referred to the same people. Heading each local group was its oldest member.[9] He or she provided the leadership that enabled members to work together to plant, cultivate, and harvest.

Society in ancient China was sustained by a system of values that emphasized *social order, ethical conduct, and fulfilling one's responsibilities to others*. These values guided people's daily activities within a clearly understood hierarchy,[10] at the top of which was the group's oldest member, a grandparent or parent of many group members. His or her authority extended into all areas of life, not merely agricultural production.

For the Chinese villager, social approval came to those who emphasized *the group's* welfare more than their own unique desires and needs.[11] These shared virtues and ways of life were the day-to-day, decade-to-decade experience of millions of villagers in China and, to some extent, throughout much of Asia across more than 5,000 years.

Confucius Highlights Existing Virtues

We rarely use the word "sage" anymore, but it nicely describes Confucius. Raised in poverty during the 6th century BCE, Confucius is now known in China as *Kǒngfūzǐ* ("Master Kong").

Asian values and ways of life did not originate with Confucius. At the time he was born, the Chinese had been living a village- and clan-focused, agricultural lifestyle for some 3,000 years; their ways of life were well established. (In his *Analects*, Confucius calls himself "the transmitter who invented nothing.")[12] Using memorable ways of teaching such as anecdotes and proverbs, he strengthened existing values. He also added his own emphases.

One virtue that Confucius emphasized was *rén*, meaning benevolence or kindness. He held that a Good person acts to benefit his group, including his extended group in the wider society, not merely his local village, clan, or family.

One story told about Confucius is that a disciple said to him: "Master, is there any one word that could guide a person throughout life?" Confucius replied, "How about *reciprocity*! Never impose on others what you would not choose for yourself."[13]

So how does one gain sterling qualities such as empathy and a capacity for reciprocity?

If an American decides to gain more empathy, he'll probably try to put himself mentally "in the shoes of" others, to appreciate their points of view. For Confucius, that wasn't enough.

Another virtue to which Confucius gave high importance was the gaining of knowledge through study. In those days, to study meant to master ancient Chinese classics. Confucius thought the classics contained valuable insights and deep thinking that would lead people to wisdom, reciprocity, and virtue. In his *Analects*, Confucius wrote, "Review the old to understand the new; thus one can become a master."[14]

Confucius also thought that *anyone* could master the classics, regardless of any factor—including native intelligence. An equal-opportunity teacher, Confucius assumed that the great equalizer among students would be persistent hard work, which the less intelligent students would apply in greater measure.

Influence of the Imperial Examinations[15]

Over 1,000 years after the death of Confucius, an Imperial Examination System was established in China. Its purpose was to identify the most able individuals to hold the senior administrative posts under the emperor. Eventually, similar systems were adopted by Korea and Vietnam, and to a lesser extent by Japan. In the mid-1800s, even British leaders became so impressed with the Chinese system that they instituted open, competitive exams for top civil service posts.

Try to recall the most grueling exam you ever took. Compare it with this: The Chinese exam-taker studied and prepared for *years*. At the examination site, he was searched for hidden printed materials, then admitted to a tiny room containing a simple bed and desk. He took with him his bedding, chamber pot, water pitcher, food, and writing materials. There he remained for three days and two nights. No interruptions. No communication with anyone. The pass rate was around 5%. For the highest level exam, it was 2%.

Confucian ideals influenced the imperial exams, which mainly tested candidates' precise memory of long stretches of admired Chinese classic texts. Almost any male could take these exams regardless of his social status (women were admitted in 1853). Many exam-takers were from relatively wealthy families, who could support their sons through years of constant study and tutoring. Sometimes poor families would pool their resources to support an especially promising relative. Even those who failed gained prestige as learned men in their local regions.

A little more than 100 years have passed since the Imperial Examination System was abolished. It had lasted for exactly 1,300 years. It was a powerful force unifying the vast stretches of China, both politically and in terms of Chinese people's values and aspirations. We need to keep this in mind as we ponder how today's East Asian students prepare for and perform on exams.

Key differences between ancient China and ancient Greece are summarized by figure 7.1.

EXPLAINING EAST ASIANS' DRIVE TO LEARN

In the preface to this book, readers were advised to expect that decades of research would show that, when compared with American children, East Asian children are more receptive to school learning. Finally, we have enough information to understand why that's true.

Two of the deepest reasons why East Asians are more receptive to school learning are that . . .

Ten differences between ancient China and ancient Greece	
Ancient China	**Ancient Greece**
1. Vast regions ruled by imperial dynasties.	1. Many small, independent city-states.
2. Economic base is village-level agriculture.	2. Economic base is herding and fishing.
3. Village farm activities need coordination.	3. Tiny garden plots need no coordination.
4. Public decisions made by senior member.	4. Public decisions made by citizen group.
5. People's thinking is group-influenced.	5. People expect to disagree and debate.
6. People are respectful of the hierarchy.	6. People often may decide for themselves.
7. Group-focused reciprocity is expected.	7. Self-focused individualism is respected.
8. Relationships confined to village, clan.	8. Relations possible beyond one's group.
9. Gaining knowledge is key path to virtue.	9. Gaining knowledge is practically useful.
10. Top exam mark leads to power, wealth.	10. Top exam mark gains admiration or envy.

Figure 7.1.

- their ways of life have many characteristics of a "communitarian" society, a type known to support a culture of learning in which *children are expected to be attentive and receptive to learning opportunities*, even those not deliberately intended for them (Discovery Step 6); and
- their 5,000+ years of history, including Confucian teachings and the Imperial Examination System, has conditioned them to view deep knowledge as personally transformative, and therefore to view *a learner's mastery of knowledge as a virtuous act* (this Discovery Step).

Note the word "mastery." It's not a word you hear often in American educational circles, where the word of choice is "proficiency." Proficiency is pretty darn good. Mastery is *perfection*.

Note the word "virtuous." It's not a word you hear often among Americans of any kind. We talk about school learning as having practical value. We think of it as helping a young person grasp how the world works, and figure out how he can make his way in the world. It's *useful*!

But here's the thing: For us, school learning will be useful at some future time. For East Asians, school learning *and* the effort it requires are virtuous . . . *right now*. Learning and the effort to learn are moral and social imperatives.

They're not just Good Ideas. They're not merely an Asian tradition. The drive to learn is *important to a family's identity*, part of its claim on others' respect and, thus, necessary for members' social as well as career advancement.

When learning is deeply embedded in a family's sense of Who It Is, learning becomes infused with emotion. Children from such families arrive at the schoolhouse door *receptive to learning*.

Perhaps Dr. Jin Li's *hào xúe xīn* captures it best: "Heart and mind for wanting to learn." But since that's not how Americans talk, this book's title is *The Drive to Learn*.

HOW STEP 7 ADVANCED OUR DISCOVERY PROCESS

We began by wondering whether historical factors help explain East Asians' fervent drive to learn. We found that David Lancy, an authority on children worldwide, has concluded that children everywhere are prone to resist group learning in classrooms. Their resistance must be *overcome* or *prevented*. Starting from that point, we gained these historical perspectives:

- From an early age, American children expect to have their preferences taken into account. Their behavior reflects the Western tradition of individualism, traceable to ancient Greece. For them to learn in classroom groups, their individualism must be temporarily neutralized.
- Here in the United States (and in the Western world generally), the emphasis has been on *overcoming* children's resistance to classroom learning. From ancient times until the early 20th century, using the "stick" was common. Recently, using "carrots" became an often-used method.
- From an early age, East Asian children are adapted to live within cultures that value social order, reciprocity, and respect for hierarchy. They become accustomed to thinking and acting in the interests of their group, and to fulfilling responsibilities to others.
- Confucius, a Chinese sage venerated by many, emphasized the above values and mindsets. He also taught that *mastering* ancient texts enabled anyone to gain wisdom and virtue. The Chinese Imperial Examinations strengthened his emphasis on learning all the way to *mastery*.
- In East Asia, these historical factors combined to make mastery learning and the effort to attain it *virtuous* and *important to family identity*. In this way, children's resistance to learning in groups is *prevented*. Children arrive at school relatively *receptive* to classroom learning.

Given that East Asian children arrive at the schoolhouse door relatively receptive to school learning, what are their parents' *assumptions* about the "how" of raising children? And what are some of their parents' *practical techniques* for raising their children? We'll address the first of those questions in Discovery Step 8, the second in Discovery Step 9.

FURTHER READING

If you'd like more detail about the researchers' findings, or simply wish to know what inspired the contents of Discovery Step 7, read the following entries in the annotated bibliography at www.thedrivetolearn.info.

- Fong, Ricci W., & Man Tak Yuen (2016). The role of self-efficacy and connectedness in the academic success of Chinese learners.
- Gross-Loh, Christine (2015). *Parenting without Borders: Surprising Lessons Parents around the World Can Teach Us* (especially chapter 7, High pressure? What Asian learning looks like).
- Lancy, David F. (2015). *The Anthropology of Childhood* (2nd ed.).
- Lee, Wing On (1996). The cultural context for Chinese learners: Conceptions of learning in the Confucian tradition.
- Li, Jin (2003). U.S. and Chinese cultural beliefs about learning.
- Stafford, Charles (1995). *The Roads of Childhood: Learning and Identification in Angang.*
- Tweed, Roger B., & Darrin R. Lehman (2002). Learning considered within a cultural context: Confucian and Socratic approaches.
- van Egmond, Marieke C., et al. (2013). Mind and virtue: The meaning of learning, a matter of culture.

Chapter Eight

Discovery Step 8: Revealing How Parents Think

What Are East Asian Parents' Assumptions about How to Raise Children?

In her engaging 2013 book, *The Smartest Kids in the World*, Amanda Ripley follows three American exchange students during the 2010–2011 school year as they encounter differences in, respectively, Finland, Poland, and Korea. Eric, 18 years old and from Minnesota, spent his year in Busan, Korea. One day, Eric learned that his host brother's Nintendo DS had been confiscated by his host mother because she caught him playing with the console before he'd finished his homework. Here's how Ripley portrays Eric's reaction to this discovery:[1]

> When it came to education, Eric's host mother did not send mixed messages. She cooked dinner for her kids every night and worked hard to make every opportunity available to them; but on the subject of studying, she did not negotiate. They had to work hard—especially in English—and school took priority over everything else.
>
> She . . . dealt with her own kids the way a coach might treat his star players. Her job was to train those kids, to push them, and even bench them to prove a point. Her job was not to protect them from strain.
>
> From what Eric had seen, his host mom was not unusual. Most Korean parents saw themselves as coaches, while American parents tended to act more like cheerleaders.

This excerpt previews the principal conclusion that will be reached in this Discovery Step.

THE OUTWARD FOCUS OF THE EAST ASIAN FAMILY

Were you surprised to read that this section is about the *outward* focus of East Asian families? That's appropriate. So far, much has been made of East Asian families' unity, commonality, and shared sense of "self." So it's easy to imagine them as turned inward. They're not.

The East Asian family is turned outward because it is keenly aware of its reputation and standing—its virtue, honor, or "face"—among other families within its community.[2] This is to be expected in any community with historical roots in the ways of life of a society grounded in *community interdependence*. A hallmark of such societies is the key role of social competence: fitting in, getting along, cooperating, and respecting the hierarchy. These ways of life arose long ago when community cooperation had survival value—literally!

In communities where these values are strong, how others evaluate your family is critical. Yes, we Americans care about what others think. But societies that are grounded in community interdependence surpass us: Caring what others think has a sense of urgency. And the attention of others in the community is focused far more on families and clans, far less on individuals.

So the question becomes: How do a family's children fit into this picture?

Children as a Family's Representatives

Again it's worth noting that American parents are not strangers to caring about what others think about their children. The difference is a matter of emphasis.

In the United States, people think of a child as a unique individual with inborn aptitudes and traits who happens to be a family member. If the child is worthy of praise, it's mostly for his personal qualities; his parents get some reflected glory. If he's worthy of blame, it's primarily for his personal deficiencies, some of which are believed to be fixed and beyond his parents' control.

In East Asia, people assume that a child is a *representative* of her family. They know she's an individual, but she's not viewed as unique and eventually separate. If she's worthy of praise, the family is being praised. If she's worthy of blame, all members suffer embarrassment. Her inborn aptitudes and traits don't matter—they're malleable. The standing of the family and it's virtue in the eyes of others depends on each member. She is a member.

When every family member is accountable for the family's standing in the eyes of others, the dynamic that drives child-rearing is different from what we Americans regard as normal.

TWO APPROACHES TO RAISING CHILDREN

When it comes to the "how" of raising children, Americans and East Asians work from different playbooks. The critical differences can be found in each playbook's contrasting *assumptions* about children's development, how they learn best, and what their roles should be. Beginning with Discovery Step 3, this book has revealed these sets of assumptions. Figure 8.1 summarizes many of the assumptions already covered plus a few being mentioned here for the first time.

Nine assumptions about children and child-raising	
East Asians	**Americans**
1. A newborn arrives with abilities that are malleable through effort & perseverance.	1. A newborn arrives with inborn potential to become a person with unique traits.
2. A child's basic role is as an apprentice or novice who is learning the family's ways & values so she represents it well.	2. A child's basic role is as an equal and increasingly autonomous family member who is learning how to be self-sufficient.
3. To fit into family & community, a child needs deliberate instruction and training.	3. To be helped to identify his potential, a child needs a variety of experiences.
4. To fit into family & community, a child must build a sense of connectedness.	4. To identify his potential and gain social skills, a child must build a sense of self.
5. To be socially skilled, a child must learn to respond to others' needs & emotions.	5. To be socially skilled, a child must learn to advocate for his own needs & ideas.
6. To help maintain her family's standing, a child must diligently pursue knowledge.	6. To make his family proud, a child must show progress in realizing his potential.
7. To become an adept learner, a child must be receptive to the knowledge of experts.	7. To become an adept learner, a child must learn to explore & discover on his own.
8. A key role of parents is to directly ensure that their child acquires knowledge.	8. A key role of parents is to support their child's realization of his own potential.
9. A child demonstrates virtue by studying diligently and gaining social competence.	9. A child meets expectations by gaining mental acuity and excelling in *some* way.

Figure 8.1.

Anthropologists study humans by observing details. They also summarize their findings, Big Picture style. Here are a few of the two playbooks' assumptions about the raising of children.

The Facilitative Approach of Americans[3]

The American approach is facilitative. The arrival of a newborn gives parents the opportunity to facilitate the emergence into adulthood of a unique person with optimized potentials. At birth, these potentials aren't known (What will he end up being good at?), so they must be identified, then developed. In addition, it's important for the child to become socially adept, to make many friends, to learn to use his mind effectively, and, in general, to become "well rounded."

For all this to happen, he must be nurtured, protected from danger, and introduced to a wide range of experiences. As facilitators, his parents marshal resources, arrange opportunities, and watch for emerging interests and abilities, which they then foster. Yes, they occasionally insist that something be done, or not done. But most American parents do not authoritatively direct and mold their offspring. They facilitate their offspring's emergence into adulthood.

What potentials do the parents *hope* will emerge? Although most want their child to do well in school, they aren't hoping that he'll blossom into an academic star and future scholar.

In Discovery Step 3, we noted that one anthropologist concluded that Americans emphasize *self-enhancement*. Now we're in a better place to grasp his meaning. It's about the assumption that any person's combination of traits and skills is very largely the outcome of potentials acquired at birth, which should be enhanced. A key role of parents is to facilitate the enhancement process.

The Supervisory Approach of East Asians[4]

The East Asian approach is supervisory. The arrival of a newborn presents parents with an unformed and *malleable* being over whose final shape her parents can, *and should*, have major influence. They feel that it's imperative for her to learn how to be a person who fits into the family and maintains, or (even better!) increases, its standing in the eyes of others. Of little or no concern are her inborn potentials. Of intense concern are her connectedness with the family and her *learning how* to learn, to complete tasks the right way, and eventually to excel on her own.

So the parents take charge. They supervise her development. They authoritatively mold her values, her behavior, and her capacity to excel. But in what ways should she excel? The child's wishes may play a role, but the decision is made by her supervisors. They know what's admired in their community; they foresee what's likely to serve her well as an adult. So the parents shape her, actively and deliberately. The child becomes *receptive* to their shaping, understanding it as the way in which her parents express their love and care.

East Asian parents commonly expect their child to gain the drive to learn and thus to excel academically. Their intention, infused with emotional fervor, is a central aspect of the family's "self"—thus, of her own self. Doing this is her responsibility to her family. If she both attains academic exceptionality and does so via hard work and perseverance, she doubly enhances the family's standing, reputation, and "face."

The anthropologist I quoted earlier concluded that East Asians emphasize *self-improvement*. That's based on the assumption that people are malleable, first at the hands of their parents, older siblings, and other knowledgeable adults; thereafter through their own efforts. Each individual's objective is to keep on improving through lifelong learning and self-cultivation, hopefully to the point where he or she becomes *exceptional*[5]—outstanding or extraordinary.

Self-improvement begins, and becomes ingrained, under the supervision of one's parents.

HOW THE CHINESE TALK ABOUT PARENTING

A California-based researcher who devoted years to understanding parenting East and West knew that, for Americans, "child-rearing" was a positive term. Being Chinese herself, she also knew that, for the Chinese, *jiāoxùn* [pronounced *jow shun*] was a positive term. As a verb, *jiāo* means "to teach, instruct"; as a noun, *xùn* means "example, model." "Child-*training*" is the best English translation of *jiāoxùn*.[6] (Its meaning, she quipped, refers to a level of maternal involvement that's beyond what most American mothers think wise—or have the patience to provide.)[7]

This same researcher emphasized *gŭan* [pronounced *gwahn*]. *Gŭan* means "to be in charge of; to manage; to take care of, administer; to govern, control." These meanings suggest the responsibilities of a manager or supervisor. When applied to parenting, *gŭan* implies a deeply caring manager, not a coolly detached one. Here's how two anthropologists explained *jiāoxùn* and *gŭan*:[8]

> Loving your child, you want to train him properly for a future educational career, *and the child must accept the parent's instructions*. This starts early, with mothers engaging in a form of didactic guidance that seems domineering. . . . This style is also evident in didactic routines designed to train the young children for school performance, including the use of flash cards.

Most Americans will find this take-charge, training-focused, managerial view of parenting distasteful. They believe that parents should relate to their children with protective support and esteem-expanding love, not managerial efficiency!

But as we've seen before, East Asians harbor different basic assumptions, from which come different child-raising priorities. Given their assumptions, Chinese parents' "how" gives priority to attentively molding their child's behavior; guaranteeing that she applies persistent effort and masters her studies; and ensuring that, as a representative of their family, she excels usually if not always. These priorities call for a high degree of participatory control, caretaking, and training. They call for *gŭan*. For a Chinese parent, *that's how love is demonstrated*.[9]

But wait! The children loathe all this parental command and control, right? Don't many children emerge psychologically damaged from their parents' authoritarian suppression?

That's *not* what research has shown. Instead, it has repeatedly shown that the great majority of Chinese children feel their parents' *jiāoxùn* and *gŭan* as evidence of warmth, care, and devotion to their well-being and eventual success as adults. Americans' hand-wringing about psychological damage arises from our belief that children are weak, fragile beings.[10]

Summing up several investigations of *gŭan*-style parenting in Western societies as well as in China, Japan, and Korea, one researcher concluded that all those studies . . .[11]

> found that *gŭan* was strongly and positively associated [by the Chinese children] with warmth. They also found that *gŭan* was only weakly associated with restrictive or hostile control. In North America and Germany, parental control was found to be associated with perceived parental hostility and rejection; but in Japan and Korea the same behaviors were associated with perceived parental warmth and acceptance. [One researcher] stressed that "Japanese adolescents even feel *rejected* by their parents when they experience only little control and a broader range of autonomy."

HOW THE JAPANESE TALK ABOUT PARENTING

The Japanese have many terms for child development and parental supervision.[12] We'll examine only five of them,[13] which will give us a sense of where Japanese priorities lie.

The first is *seken*, "world, public, society." This Discovery Step began by noting the outward focus of East Asian families. That's what *seken* is about. Japanese mothers are keenly aware of whomever is likely to be watching her child's abilities and behavior develop—not to mention her own mothering skills! Kinfolk, neighbors, teachers, acquaintances, shopkeepers, other parents—they're all part of one's community, one's *seken*, where other people are watching and judging.

The second is *shitsuke* [three syllables: *she-tsu-ke*, but the second is barely voiced], which refers to the rearing of young children.[14] Among its definitions are training and discipline; longer definitions invariably imply a take-charge role by the parents. For example, a Japanese dictionary of folklore says that *shitsuke* is . . .[15]

> the putting into the body of a child the arts of living and good manners in order to create one grown-up person [literally, one portion of a social person].

An English anthropologist who studied how the Japanese socialize children wrote that . . .[16]

> in most cases Japanese caretakers do not wait for these things to happen naturally. They carefully guide the child in the "proper" way to do things, *often through clearly defined physical aid*, and the child learns to impose a cultural order on its physical development.

Third, a good child in Japan is *sunao*, often translated as "obedient"—which gives Americans a mistaken impression. Properly understood, *sunao* means nonresistant, open-minded, authentic in intent, and cooperative in spirit.[17] A respected Japanese psychologist once explained *sunao* as meaning amenable[18] (responsive, accommodating). Translating *sunao* as obedient suggests that the child is self-negating. Actually, *sunao* means that the child is self-*affirming* through her cooperation with others. A *sunao* child expresses her essence through willing, collaborative teamwork, suggesting that her goals are identical to the others' goals.

Fourth, the main way a good child acquires positive traits and abilities is via *gambaru*, "to persist, to not give up." Japanese teachers, in response to parents' concern about how their child can attain top marks, typically respond, "I think a little more *gambaru* would be good."[19] As we've seen in Discovery Step 4, learning in East Asia isn't only about attaining a worthy goal (a top exam mark). It's equally about *how* you attained it: through hard work and perseverance.

Finally, among parents a common expression is *Kurō saseta hō ga ii*, "It's better to make (the child) endure difficulties." Meaning suffering or hardship, *kurō* is believed to be good for children, stripping away self-centeredness and hastening maturity. *Kurō* is never a parental punishment. It can result from all sorts of naturally occurring situations, including a need for unrelenting study.

When *kurō* strikes, the parents are right there, participating with their child shoulder-to-shoulder in a collaborative effort to overcome the challenge.

CHEERLEADERS AND COACHES

At the start of this Discovery Step, Eric, an American student in Korea, concluded that Korean parents saw themselves as coaches while American parents acted more like cheerleaders. The more we know about child-rearing in the United States and East Asia, the more apt that comparison becomes!

Imagine a high school sport. The athletes are learning to play; their goal is to perform well and win often. The cheerleaders encourage the players. The coaches ensure that the players *know how to* play well. Consider these different modes of support:

Cheerleaders' main functions and activities are to . . .

- be present during games, remaining on the sidelines.
- demonstrate enthusiasm for team success, encouraging the crowd to do likewise.
- build players' confidence in whatever levels of competence they have.
- regard a team win with joy; regard a team loss with self-esteem-boosting reassurance.
- between games, work on their own group's routines.

Coaches' main functions and activities are to . . .

- be present during both practice sessions and games, remaining on the sidelines.
- demonstrate enthusiasm for team success, encouraging the players privately.
- direct the players in strategies and tactics for winning the game at hand.
- set and enforce rules for player health and behavior to support competency development.
- strengthen players' determination to persevere in improving their levels of competence.
- demonstrate proper playing techniques based on their own prior mastery.
- provide models, then drill the players again and again to ensure mastery.
- directly criticize each player's techniques, analyze errors, drill, and retrain.
- discipline players who don't work hard, obey rules, pay attention, or master basics.

Discovery Step 8: Revealing How Parents Think 77

- regard team success or failure as *their own personal* success or failure.
- have their own worth evaluated by others in terms of the team's success or failure.

Finally, most players will be *receptive* to their coaches' expertise and instruction, *and* to their caring, mentorship, and side-by-side involvement in pursuing high playing competence.

HOW STEP 8 ADVANCED OUR DISCOVERY PROCESS

We came into this Discovery Step determined to understand the assumptions that East Asian parents make about the raising of children. The most important facts that emerged were these:

- An East Asian family is keenly aware, as a family unit or clan, of its reputation and standing—its virtue, honor, or "face"—among other clans and families with whom it has relationships.
- Each child represents the family as much as any other member. So it's vital that each child learns how to fit in, behave, study, and perform in ways that burnish her family's standing. By being receptive to the guidance of older family members, each child learns *how*.
- Each child is assumed to be a malleable being over whose final shape her parents should, and can, have great influence. So parents directly, even physically, guide, mold, and offer models for her performance. They don't merely applaud her efforts; they *actively participate with her*.
- Parents expect their child to do extremely well academically; it's her responsibility to the family. If she does so by working long and hard, she doubly enhances the family's standing.
- To describe the role of Chinese parents, "child-*training*" is more accurate than "child-rearing." The take-charge Chinese approach is captured by *gŭan*—purposefully managing or supervising the child's development with deep dedication. In Japanese, *shitsuke* has a similar meaning.
- In short, East Asian parents behave far more like coaches, far less like cheerleaders.

Now we'd like to discover those parents' practical approaches to raising—no, to *coaching* and *training*—their children. Discovery Step 9 will provide some descriptions.

FURTHER READING

If you'd like more detail about the researchers' findings, or simply wish to know what inspired the contents of Discovery Step 8, read the following entries in the annotated bibliography at www.thedrivetolearn.info.

- Chao, Ruth K. (1995). Chinese and European American cultural models of the self, reflected in mothers' childrearing beliefs.
- Chao, Ruth K., & Stanley Sue (1996). Chinese parental influence on their children's school success.
- Chao, Ruth K., & Vivian Tseng (2002). Parenting in Asia.
- Chen, Chuansheng, & David H. Uttal (1988). Cultural values, parents' beliefs, and children's achievement in the United States and China.
- Cheng, Rebecca Wing-yi, et al. (2016). Motivation of Chinese learners: An integration of etic and emic approaches.
- Fong, Ricci W., & Man Tak Yuen (2016). The role of self-efficacy and connectedness in the academic success of Chinese learners.
- Fu, Alyssa S., & Hazel Rose Markus (2014). My mother and me: Why tiger mothers motivate Asian Americans but not European Americans.
- Fung, Heidi (1999). Becoming a moral child: The socialization of shame among young Chinese children.
- Gross-Loh, Christine (2015). *Parenting without Borders: Surprising Lessons Parents around the World Can Teach Us* (especially chapter 7, "High pressure? What Asian learning looks like").
- Hendry, Joy (1986). *Becoming Japanese: The World of the Pre-School Child*.
- Hess, Robert D., & Hiroshi Azuma (1991). Cultural support for schooling: Contrasts between Japan and the United States.
- Holloway, Susan D. (1988). Concepts of ability and effort in Japan and the United States.
- Kim, Uichol, & Soo-Hyang Choi (1994). Individualism, collectivism, and child development: A Korean perspective.
- Lancy, David F. (2015). *The Anthropology of Childhood* (2nd ed.).
- Lebra, Takie Sugiyama (1994). Mother and child in Japanese socialization.
- Park, Young-Shin, & Uichol Kim (2006). Family, parent-child relationship, and academic achievement in Korea.
- Pomerantz, Eva M., et al. (2011). Changes in early adolescents' sense of responsibility to parents in the United States and China: Implications for academic functioning.
- Salili, Farideh (1996). Accepting personal responsibility for learning.
- Salzman, Mark (1986). *Iron & Silk*.

- Simons, Carol (1981). The education mother (*kyōiku mama*).
- Stevenson, Harold, & Shin-Ying Lee (1990). Contexts for achievement: A study of American, Chinese, and Japanese children.
- Stevenson, Harold W., & James W. Stigler (1992). *The Learning Gap: Why Our Schools Are Failing and What We Can Learn from Japanese and Chinese Education*.
- White, Merry I., & Robert A. LeVine (1986). What is an *ii ko* (good child)?
- Wu, David Y. H. (1996). Parental control: Psychocultural interpretations of Chinese patterns of socialization.
- Wu, Peixia, et al. (2002). Similarities and differences in mothers' parenting of preschoolers in China and the United States.

Chapter Nine

Discovery Step 9: Revealing What Parents Do

What Are East Asian Parents' Approaches to Coaching and Training Their Children?

A few years ago, an American anthropologist did something quite unusual. Instead of devoting months to studying people in groups, she devoted months—15 of them—to studying just one individual: a Japanese boy.[1] Why was "Seiji" worthy of so much attention?

About seven years previously, after Seiji had completed preschool in Japan, he relocated with his parents and a younger sister from Japan to Michigan. During the family's five-and-a-half years in Michigan, Seiji attended "Lakeview Elementary" during weekdays as well as a Japanese supplementary school for a full day every Saturday. Then the family returned to Japan, where Seiji entered the sixth grade at the "Kaichi Elementary." The anthropologist followed Seiji during the time when his family was leaving Michigan and settling back into life in Japan.

During a conversation the week before Seiji was to finish sixth grade at Kaichi, Seiji compared his experiences as a student first at Lakeview, then at Kaichi:[2]

> *Seiji:* Yeah, but Lakeview, it was better than here. You were more free, kind of. You didn't really have to really, really do it.
>
> *Anthropologist:* What do you mean? Give me an example.
>
> *Seiji:* Lakeview, if you, maybe, not really do a good job you will be fine, and at Kaichi you have to do really well even if you didn't like or you weren't good at that subject.

That is one of the most important things we're learning through this discovery process.

MAINTAIN VERY HIGH EXPECTATIONS . . . CONSISTENTLY

Seiji reported encountering higher expectations from Japanese teachers than from American teachers. East Asian *parents* similarly have higher expectations than Americans.

Maintain *Very* High Expectations

Consider this study:[3] Researchers asked mothers in the United States and China to imagine that their child took a math test with 100 possible points and an average score of 75. They were asked: What score do you expect your child to get? With what score would you be satisfied?

Both sets of mothers expected their child to receive 80 to 85 points. American mothers said they'd be satisfied with a score that was, on average, *seven points lower* than that. Chinese mothers would be satisfied with a score that was, on average, *ten points higher* than that.[4]

In both countries, both fathers and mothers were asked to rate their satisfaction with their child's school performance on a 1–5 scale on which 5 meant "very satisfied." Among Chinese mothers, 36% chose either 4 or 5; among American mothers, 76% chose either 4 or 5. Fathers? Of the Chinese dads, 28% chose 4 or 5; of the American dads, a whopping 88% chose 4 or 5.[5] So regardless of how well their child was performing, most Americans felt satisfied.[6]

Maintain Very High Expectations *Consistently*

Several research efforts revealed that East Asian and American parents have different trajectories of concern with their children's academic performance, as shown in figure 9.1.[7]

At around age 6, East Asian parents focus their child's attention on the momentous business of academic learning. This is her role and responsibility. But her family doesn't only expect this of her; they intervene and participate with her (more on this later in the chapter). In contrast, when an American child enters primary school, his parents tend to pull back; cognitive growth is now up to his teachers.

When an East Asian child leaves primary school, her habit of persevering in her studies is usually well established; her parents reduce their coaching and training—but *not* their high expectations. In the United States, the postprimary child often is reducing whatever academic focus he had and is aligning with his peers. His parents try to counter this . . . but now it's an uphill battle!

Trajectories of concern with the child's academic performance		
East Asian parents	Time period	**American parents**
Little or no concern about cognitive or academic issues; the child is indulged.	Birth until about age 6	Efforts to jump-start cognitive growth to give the child a head start in life.
Consistently strong concern about the child's academic performance; parents become dedicated coaches and trainers.	Primary school years	Parents pull back, assuming that the school will foster cognitive growth; they shift into a cheerleader role.
Parents pull back, confident that the child's persevering study habits have been set; usually, they are correct.	Post-primary school years	Seeing their child's middling grades and openness to peer pressure, many parents ratchet up their active concern.

Figure 9.1.

One study of Japanese, Chinese (from Taiwan), and American mothers found evidence for these trajectories between the first and fifth grades.[8] When their children were first graders, the mothers were asked how satisfied they were with their child's academic performance. "Very satisfied" was selected by nearly 50% of the Americans, but by under 5% of the Chinese and Japanese. When their children were in fifth grade, "very satisfied" was the choice of nearly 35% of the Americans. But the East Asians remained down at 5% or less.

"Not satisfied" was a choice, too. When their children were first graders, "not satisfied" was the choice of around 10% of the Americans, while the East Asians were at or well above 20%. When their children were in fifth grade, "not satisfied" was chosen again by around 10% of the Americans, but it had increased to around 40% of the East Asians. The researchers wrote:[9]

> Chinese and Japanese mothers were more likely than American mothers to adopt *successively higher* criteria for their children's academic performance as their children become older. The American mothers tended to relax their standards.

Allow Self-Esteem to Grow *Intrinsically*

In the 1970s, authorities began claiming that low self-esteem was at the root of mental and social problems, and that raising children's self-esteem would boost their academic performance. Many American parents became unfailingly positive toward their children, praising them often. A common rationale was that praise prevents a child from doubting his own inborn abilities.

East Asian parents never boarded the self-esteem bandwagon. One research team studied American and Taiwanese mothers' beliefs regarding self-esteem. Since Chinese has no exactly equivalent term, in Taiwan the team used one that means "self-confidence-heart/mind." The team found that American mothers "could not talk about childrearing without talking about self-esteem." Only a few Taiwanese mothers talked about "self-confidence-heart/mind." Those who did wanted their child to *not* have very much of it, because they believed it leads to "frustration [in the face of failure], stubbornness, and unwillingness to listen and be corrected."[10]

From the East Asian perspective, when a child falters academically, preserving her self-esteem isn't useful. What's useful is diagnosis, more persistent effort on her part, and more direct assistance from her coach. Side-by-side, parent and child strive for a superior outcome.

The only worthwhile self-esteem is that felt *when one's goal has been attained*. When that occurs, parental praise isn't needed. Self-esteem wells up *inside*, intrinsically and organically.

INTERVENE TO ENSURE THAT HIGH EXPECTATIONS ARE MET

East Asian parents *intervene and participate* to support their child's high academic performance. Yes, this requires time, energy, and persistence. What does it look like on a day-to-day basis?

Govern the Child's Use of Time

When mastery and the effort to attain it are a top family priority, things happen that would be unusual in American families. Other things *don't* happen that are typical of American families.

The most famous—or infamous—list of things that *don't* happen in such a family is the one found on the first page of the widely debated 2011 book by Amy Chua, *Battle Hymn of the Tiger Mother*. Writes Chua, "Here are some things my daughters . . . were never allowed to do":[11]

- attend a sleepover
- have a playdate
- be in a school play
- watch TV or play computer games
- choose their own extracurricular activities
- get any grade less than an A

Some Americans thought this was over the top. But what cannot be doubted is that Chua's list is heading in the right direction. For if academic *mastery*—not mere proficiency—is the goal, then the daily life of one's child simply cannot be like that of most other American children.

A little-noticed book on East Asian–style parenting is *Top of the Class*,[12] by Korean American sisters, one a physician, one an attorney. Describing their day-to-day routine as youngsters, they reveal their constant focus and their parents' interventions:[13]

> Our parents managed our time after school so well. . . . [After we relaxed for about an hour], our mother would sit down with us at the dining-room table as we discussed any upcoming tests and/or assignments that were due. For the next hour and a half (with one ten-minute break), we would complete all our homework.
>
> [After dinner], we would resume another one to two hours of "study time." Activities during this time would . . . go far beyond what was expected: we might get a head start on our summer reading list or attempt to learn concepts beyond what our homework assignments might have tested. Our father always loved to check our homework, after which he would make up five or ten much more difficult questions for us to answer, just to make sure we truly understood.

Be Generous in Contributing *Your* Time

Consider *The Hybrid Tiger*, a book written in 2014 by a Chinese immigrant[14] who was very critical of Amy Chua's tiger mothering. Yet even he stated that "Chinese [parenting] is *very* different from American parenting," and suggested that an American parent . . .[15]

- pay much more attention to your children's school education
- sacrifice more for your children's education
- involve yourself in your children's studying

Concerning "sacrifice," in the index of *The Hybrid Tiger*, "sacrifice" has 32 entries, far more than any other term (the next highest number, 23, is for "to win"). In the book's section titled "Chinese Parents and 'Sacrifice,'" the author tells of a time when he and his wife carpooled with another Chinese couple, parents of an upper elementary pupil, on their way to a banquet:[16]

> [I] noticed that Leslie [his friend's wife] was reading a rather large book.
>
> "Is that a textbook?" I asked her.
>
> "Yes," Leslie said, looking up. "It's my son's. I'm reading his assignment. I'll go over it with him later tonight after the banquet."

"Do you mean the homework that he's done?" I asked, confused. "You're reading something he wrote?"

"No, no, no," she said. "I'm reading what he was supposed to read. His homework. We do it together. He reads it, and then I read it, too, so that I can understand and help him with his work if he needs it."

"Ah," I said. "I see. But he's not struggling at school, is he?"

"No, he's getting all A's."

That's a wonderful illustration of a child's coach and trainer doing her East Asian thing!

By the way, East Asian parents devote little or no time to supporting the child's *school*. Parent-teacher conferences? Always present. Other school events? Rarely present.[17]

Participate with and Directly Instruct the Child

In earlier Discovery Steps, "knowing about" and "knowing how to" appeared often. That's because East Asian coaching and training emphasizes learning *how to do things correctly.*

We encountered this emphasis in Howard Gardner's story about Benjamin and the key. The Chinese who helped Benjamin put the key in the slot—by grasping his hand—exemplify the East Asian focus on children's *knowing how*. In the Chinese view, exploration and discovery waste time. Verbal pointers miss the mark. Esteem-building encouragement puts the cart before the horse (self-esteem occurs *because* a task has been mastered). Instead, the Chinese physically molded Benjamin's movements. They saw he was doing it wrong, stopped that, then trained him how to do it correctly. In doing so, they *participated with* Benjamin during his learning process.

Americans are less likely to directly guide, mold, and offer models for a child's performance. They're more likely to verbally help him grasp the nature of the task, assuming that if he *knows about* the task, his attempts to complete it will become more effective.[18] They don't want to disturb his efforts. After all, learning to act self-reliantly is very important in the United States.

One research team found evidence of these contrasting methods in mother-child pairs in which the children were 2 years old. Completed near Chicago, this study compared Japanese and American mothers.[19] The Japanese mothers had been in the United States only a short time. The research team videotaped the following situation involving the mothers and their toddlers:

In their homes, each mother-toddler pair was given a typical toy for developing a child's ability to sort shapes. Its top had differently shaped holes, and it came with differently shaped blocks. Each mother was instructed to "help [her child] complete this task as many times as possible in ten minutes." The main findings were these:

- Before the Japanese toddlers began an attempt, their mothers were much more likely to *physically assist* them. The mothers intervened so the task would be completed *together*.
- When the American toddlers began an attempt on their own, their mothers were more likely to delay assisting, or to not assist at all. They arranged for their child to act *independently*.
- The American toddlers were far more likely to spontaneously walk away from the task. When they did, their mothers were less likely to try to get them to return, compared with the Japanese mothers (in the very few instances when Japanese toddlers tried to walk away).

Another study of Japanese and American mothers throws more light on the difference between emphasizing *knowing about* versus *knowing how to*. The children were 4 years old, and the task was to sort wooden blocks of different shapes. The researchers found the amount of mother-to-child talk didn't differ. What differed was the mothers' overall approach:[20]

> The American mothers would typically teach step by step, *verbalizing* how to do it and asking for *verbal* responses. Japanese mothers would *show in a wholistic fashion* how to sort blocks, and use verbal messages to engage children to look carefully, to think better, and to do it right. The Japanese mothers do not teach verbally, but use verbalization to get the child involved.

In both of these studies, the American mothers rarely involved themselves physically in the task. They either held back so the child could act self-reliantly or engaged him in conversation about the task. The Japanese mothers took a "hands-on" approach, demonstrating and assisting.

A REVEALING STUDY OF MOTHERS AND CHILDREN

The approaches to dealing with children that we've been thinking about are illustrated by a study carried out in Hong Kong and the American Midwest.[21] Mothers and their 10-year-olds came to a research facility. Each child was asked to solve, by him- or herself, a set of puzzles. Some got easy puzzles, others got hard ones; only the researchers knew who got what.

After each child finished, a researcher entered the room, graded the answer sheet, and wrote the grade on the sheet. To children who had done well he said, "You did well." To those who didn't he said, "You didn't do too well."

He left the puzzles, and the answer sheet with the grade visible, on the table. Then he explained to both child and mother that they would be together in the room during a five-minute break, and that after the break the child (alone) would get similar puzzles to solve. He left the two in the room, where they were videotaped for five minutes.

The research team wanted to know how much the Chinese and American mothers *directly involved themselves* in the child's task, making it a shared effort. So the team counted the number of 30-second segments during which the mother involved herself. Examples of actions counted as her involvement were examining the puzzles, paying attention when the child explained them, solving a puzzle, checking her child's solutions, or instructing her child how to solve the puzzles.

A huge difference emerged between the two groups of mothers. The Chinese mothers directly involved themselves in their children's task far more often than the Americans, helping them learn *how to* solve the puzzles. The Chinese-American difference is shown in figure 9.2.[22]

Following her child's task effort	**Chinese mothers**	**American mothers**
Segments with **mothers' involvement** in her child's task [e.g., paying attention to child's explanations or checking his work]	5.19	1.51

Following the child's solo effort on a task, average number of 30-second segments in which *mothers directly involved themselves with their child* in figuring out how to complete the task.

Figure 9.2. Following her child's task effort, mother's involvement in the task.
Source: Florrie Fei-Yin Ng et al. (2007), European American and Chinese parents' responses to children's success and failure: Implications for children's responses. *Developmental Psychology, 43(5)*. Based on data on page 1249, short paragraph at top of column two; Ng et al. do not present these data in a table.

The researchers also wanted to learn how much the Chinese and American mothers *discussed the tasks* with their children.[23] So they counted the number of 30-second segments during which each mother made statements that were relevant, or irrelevant, to the puzzles.

Examples of task-*relevant* statements were, "What did you have to do?"; "These puzzles are hard!"; and "Look, these triangles have no bottoms." Examples of task-*irrelevant* statements were "That's a very nice bracelet"; "What do you want for lunch?"; and "Stop playing with that door!"

Again, a big difference emerged between the two groups of mothers. Consider first the cases in which the children had successfully solved most or all of the puzzles. Task-*relevant* statements were made much more often by the

Following her child's *success*	Chinese mothers	American mothers
Segments with **task-relevant** statements [e.g., "This triangle has no bottom."]	6.40	3.80
Segments with **task-irrelevant** statements [e.g., "What do you want for lunch?"]	5.78	7.17

Following the child's *success*, average number of 30-second segments in which mothers made one or more statements relevant or irrelevant to the task on which the child had performed well.

Figure 9.3. Following child's success, mother's task-relevant or -irrelevant statements.
Source: Florrie Fei-Yin Ng et al. (2007), European American and Chinese parents' responses to children's success and failure: Implications for children's responses. *Developmental Psychology*, 43(5). Based on data in table 4 on page 1250. The figure above uses data from that table but does not reproduce the table.

Chinese mothers. Task-*irrelevant* statements were made more often by the American mothers. These findings appear in figure 9.3.[24]

Now consider the cases in which the children had *failed* to solve most of the puzzles. Again, task-*relevant* statements were made more often by the Chinese mothers, while task-*irrelevant* statements were made more often by the Americans. These findings appear in figure 9.4.[25]

Following her child's *failure*	Chinese mothers	American mothers
Segments with **task-relevant** statements [e.g., "This triangle has no bottom."]	6.82	4.62
Segments with **task-irrelevant** statements [e.g., "What do you want for lunch?"]	5.12	6.43

Following the child's *failure*, average number of 30-second segments in which mothers made one or more statements relevant or irrelevant to the task on which the child had performed poorly.

Figure 9.4. Following child's failure, mother's task-relevant or -irrelevant statements.
Source: Florrie Fei-Yin Ng et al. (2007), European American and Chinese parents' responses to children's success and failure: Implications for children's responses. *Developmental Psychology*, 43(5). Based on data in table 4 on page 1250. The figure above uses data from that table but does not reproduce the table.

The East Asian mothers in this study intervened to participate and involve themselves in their children's tasks. The American mothers showed much less active interest in their children's tasks, even when it was clear that their prior performance had been poor.

HOW STEP 9 ADVANCED OUR DISCOVERY PROCESS

We came into this Discovery Step wanting to understand more about East Asian parents' approaches to coaching and training their children. The main approaches that we considered were these:

- East Asian parents maintain *very* high expectations for their child's academic performance.
- They maintain those very high expectations throughout the child's school years. In fact, many adopt *successively higher* criteria for academic performance as their child gets older.
- They govern their child's use of time, ensuring that a large majority of waking hours is devoted to academic learning, including learning that surpasses what teachers expect.
- They are very generous in dedicating their own time to serve as the child's coach.
- They allow the child's self-esteem to grow intrinsically as a result of objectives attained. They do not use verbal flattery to extrinsically inflate or maintain his self-esteem.
- They *participate with* their child, learning alongside him or her, jointly addressing challenges.
- They instruct, mold, and train their child, focusing on *how to accomplish tasks correctly*.

Our Discovery Process has ended. To what extent could—should—this new information change the way we do things here in the United States?

FURTHER READING

If you'd like more detail about the researchers' findings, or simply wish to know what inspired the contents of Discovery Step 9, read the following entries in the annotated bibliography at www.thedrivetolearn.info.

- Abboud, Soo Kim, & Jane Kim (2006), *Top of the Class: How Asian Parents Raise High Achievers—and How You Can Too*.
- Chao, Ruth K. (1995). Chinese and European American cultural models of the self, reflected in mothers' childrearing beliefs.
- Chao, Ruth K., & Stanley Sue (1996). Chinese parental influence on their children's school success.
- Chao, Ruth K., & Vivian Tseng (2002). Parenting in Asia.

- Chen, Chuansheng, & David H. Uttal (1988). Cultural values, parents' beliefs, and children's achievement in the United States and China.
- Chua, Amy (2011), *Battle Hymn of the Tiger Mother*.
- Damrow, Amy (2014). Navigating the structures of elementary school in the United States and Japan.
- Fogel, Alan, et al. (1992). A comparison of the parent-child relationship in Japan and the United States.
- Fu, Alyssa S., & Hazel Rose Markus (2014). My mother and me: Why tiger mothers motivate Asian Americans but not European Americans.
- Gross-Loh, Christine (2015). *Parenting without Borders: Surprising Lessons Parents around the World Can Teach Us* (especially chapter 7, "High pressure? What Asian learning looks like").
- Hess, Robert D., et al. (1986). Family influences on school readiness and achievement in Japan and the United States.
- Hess, Robert D., & Hiroshi Azuma (1991). Cultural support for schooling: Contrasts between Japan and the United States.
- Huang, Quanyu (2014). *The Hybrid Tiger: Secrets of the Extraordinary Success of Asian-American Kids*.
- Miller, Peggy J., et al. (2002). Self-esteem as folk theory: A comparison of European American and Taiwanese mothers' beliefs.
- Ng, Florrie Fei-Yin, et al. (2007). European American and Chinese parents' responses to children's success and failure: Implications for children's responses.
- Parmar, Parminder, et al. (2008). Teacher or playmate? Asian immigrant and Euro-American parents' participation in their young children's daily activities.
- Schneider, Barbara, & Yongsook Lee (1990). A model for academic success: The school and home environment of East Asian students.
- Shimahara, Nobuo K., & Akira Sakai (1995). *Learning to Teach in Two Cultures: Japan and the United States*.
- Stevenson, Harold, & Shin-Ying Lee (1990). Contexts for achievement: A study of American, Chinese, and Japanese children.
- Stevenson, Harold W., & James W. Stigler (1992). *The Learning Gap: Why Our Schools Are Failing and What We Can Learn from Japanese and Chinese Education*.
- Wang, Qi, & Michelle D. Leichtman (2000). Same beginnings, different stories: A comparison of American and Chinese children's narratives.
- Wu, Peixia, et al. (2002). Similarities and differences in mothers' parenting of preschoolers in China and the United States.

Chapter Ten

So What Should We Do?

To What Extent Could—Should—This New Information Change the Way We Do Things?

In Discovery Step 1, we briefly overviewed the findings of four types of measurement that, for decades, have been telling us that the outcomes of American education are poor:

- the findings of researchers who spend time observing inside American schools;
- the experiences of institutions that deal with high school graduates and dropouts;
- the performance of our students on domestic comparative tests; and
- the performance of our students on international comparative tests.

Now there's a new research effort on the horizon. As of this writing, only some of the details are available. Here's what we know so far:

This research was revealed in July 2016 by an article in the *New York Times*.[1] It told of an ongoing study led by Dr. Prashant Loyalka, a professor of education at Stanford University. The goal of the study is to gain a better understanding of the quality of university education in several countries, including China. In order for the researchers to understand how much students are learning at Chinese and other universities, the students' capacities as entering freshmen must first be measured. The students are all majors in electrical engineering and computer science.

Here's where it gets interesting. The study isn't looking only at Chinese university students; it's *also comparing them with Russian and American counterparts*. And it isn't measuring only the students' academic skills; it's *also measuring their critical thinking skills*.

To measure critical thinking, the researcher is using an American-made assessment.[2] Data from that assessment are revealing that,[3] *when it comes to critical thinking, Chinese freshmen appear to significantly outperform American freshmen.*[4] Russian freshmen also appear to outperform their American counterparts.

What is being measured is *critical thinking!* American educators know that critical thinking is an essential skill for students to learn. But when Chinese freshmen take a Made-in-the-USA test to measure that skill, they outperform American freshmen. We're talking about *the Chinese*! They are those unfortunate students who, at least until you read this book, were envisioned as sitting passively through boring lectures, drilling instead of learning to think independently, and repeating word-for-word on tests whatever they'd memorized without understanding.

It is findings like these that lend urgency to the question, *So what could—should—we do?*

WHAT ARE OUR OPTIONS?

This book asks, "Why do American students learn less than East Asian students?" An answer was suggested: "When compared with East Asian children, our children are *less receptive* to school learning." From that point onward, our attention has focused on discovering why East Asian children are receptive to school learning, and why they come to school with a drive to learn.

A Review of Our Discovery Findings

In order to think clearly about our options, it will be useful to review the phases of, and the findings from, the nine-step process of discovery that we've just completed.

1. We recognized the problem, then stated it as a question for which we need to find an answer.
2. We investigated popular beliefs about education in East Asia, most of which came from casual observers who considered only superficial appearances. From that point on, we relied solely on the findings of anthropologists and other trained researchers. Our investigation made us aware that East Asian students expect to gain academic understanding gradually, by applying huge amounts of time and effort. We wondered: What motivates them to do that?
3. We examined research about motivational differences. When it comes to studying and learning, East Asians appear to have a strong *inner de-*

termination with these characteristics: (a) it is enhanced, rather than undermined, by failure to learn; (b) it is not limited by a belief that people are born with fixed abilities; (c) it is similar to Carol Dweck's "growth mindset"; and (d) one of its outcomes is a consistent commitment to self-improvement.

4. To explore the foundations of this inner determination, we turned to work by Dr. Jin Li. Her findings have revealed that Americans and Chinese think about learning differently: They learn for different reasons; they approach learning tasks differently; and they expect different outcomes. Finally, and most important, Chinese (and other East Asians) associate both knowledge and the effort needed to gain it with morality. They learn in order to become human beings with admirable qualities, which will make them virtuous. This conscious intention infuses their efforts with enduring emotional energy—with "the drive to learn."

5. To further understand why people in East Asia infuse learning with emotional drive, we probed the meaning of "self" there and in the United States. Research evidence suggests that in East Asia, "self" is not about a single individual, but about her *and her family*. A child applies emotional drive to learning because that's what her family does. She and her family are deeply united on this matter; it's as though they share a single mind. The result for the child is what American psychologists call "intrinsic motivation" to study and learn.

6. We investigated the term "culture of learning." It refers to how a society's adults ensure that their children learn the right things. It also refers to what each child comes to expect of others, *and of himself*, while learning. In individualized societies, cultures of learning emphasize mental development via maturation and independent exploration. In communitarian societies, cultures of learning emphasize social development via intervention by experts (parents, older siblings, teachers). *Children learn how to be diligently receptive to caring others who have mastered whatever is to be learned.* For the most part, East Asian societies have maintained a culture of learning in which children are receptive to instruction by caring experts.

7. We also explored historical factors. Children everywhere resist classroom learning, so their resistance must be overcome or prevented. Adults in the West try to *overcome* the resistance, historically via a "stick" but recently via a "carrot." Adults in East Asia raise children to value social order, respect the hierarchy, fulfill responsibilities to others, and act in the interests of their groups. These values were refined and highlighted by Confucianism, which emphasized diligence in studying—an emphasis later stimulated by the Chinese Imperial Examinations. These factors all combined to make learning central to a family's identity, which, in turn,

prevents children's resistance in classrooms. *They are patiently receptive to being taught.*
8. To understand East Asian parents, we examined how they think. They are keenly aware of the family's standing in the eyes of others. Therefore, it's vital that each child learns *how* to fit in, behave, study, and perform in ways that burnish the family's reputation. Children are assumed to be *malleable*; parents are assumed to be rightful in directing and shaping them. Parents participate with their children; they directly instruct them; they coach and train them. The main way a child can add to her family's standing is (a) by being at or near the top of her school's academic rankings *and* (b) by visibly working long and hard to attain that goal.
9. To further understand East Asian parents, we found out what they actually *do*. They maintain very high expectations for their child's academic performance, often raising these as years pass. They govern their child's use of time, focusing it on academic learning that exceeds what her teachers expect. They are very generous in giving their time to their roles as her coaches. They never inflate their child's self-esteem, instead allowing it to grow intrinsically as the result of goals attained. They jointly address academic challenges with their child. And they *directly instruct* their child, ensuring that she learns *how to accomplish tasks correctly*.

Our Range of Options—Limited!

As those nine discovery steps have made clear, the culture of learning that characterizes most families in East Asia is fundamentally different from the one that characterizes most families in our country. The culture of learning in East Asia, a central feature of family identity, leads most East Asian students to become attentive and receptive to learning in school.

If it's vitally important for American students to become more receptive to school learning, it would seem that one option would be to use East Asian culture as a model for adapting certain aspects of our own culture. However, anyone who understands culture through study (for instance, by majoring in anthropology) or by living in two or more contrasting cultures knows this: culture becomes *very* deeply ingrained within people, who stoutly resist fundamental change.

Americans' culture of learning is not going to change because thousands of people read this book. It's not going to change because of legislation or agency mandates at the state and federal levels. It's not going to change because the adults who are in charge of public and private schools alter their policies and practices. Those "options" simply aren't realistic.

What's left? Families.

SO WHAT SHOULD *FAMILIES* DO?

Families have cultures, too—shared ways of thinking, valuing, feeling, and acting. Composed of a handful of people in face-to-face relationships, the family is best positioned to change its culture of learning in order to bring about superior outcomes for the classroom learning of its children.

But if you are an American parent, "What should my family do?" is not the first question to ask. Your first question is, "Given this new information, *should my family do anything at all?*"

It Depends on Your Priorities

There are thoughtful people who hold that, when it comes to how much our children learn in school, we Americans are perfectly fine as we are. Visible among these pundits is Dr. Diane Ravitch, the educational historian. About the international comparative tests, she writes:[5]

> Let [other nations] have the higher test scores. I prefer to bet on the creative, can-do spirit of the American people, on its character, persistence, ambition, hard work, and big dreams, none of which are ever measured or can be measured by standardized tests.

Maybe Dr. Ravitch is right. After all, *The Drive to Learn* is not about easy steps you can take to help your child get great grades. The reason East Asian students get great grades has nothing to do with easy steps! It's because their parents make assumptions, have priorities, think, behave, and use time differently from American students' parents.

Great grades are a worthwhile benefit. But the differences in parenting styles are enormous.

A strongly held goal of most American middle-class parents is for their children to become "well rounded." It's easy to see this goal being pursued by American schools, too. Most offer an amazingly wide range of courses and extracurricular activities, including a variety of sports.

An American-style well-rounded child is not the primary goal of East Asian parents. They know that mastery of academic subjects and well-roundedness cannot coexist as top priorities. Their top priority is *mastery* of the subjects taught in schools. Our top priority is well-roundedness including qualities such as independence, creativity, mental sharpness, popularity among peers, physical robustness, involvement in the community—and academic proficiency.

If your top priority for your child is academic mastery, then transform your family's culture of learning to resemble that of East Asian families. This will require bravery, for it is very likely to make your family different from others in your community.

But if this book has convinced you that you do not wish to transform your family's culture to resemble that of East Asians, then continue doing what you've been doing. (And stop saying they're smarter. East Asians ace tests because of their drive to *master* what they are learning!)

If Your Top Priority Is Mastery

If your top priority for your child is soaring academic excellence, then you'll need to invest him with the drive to learn. Fortunately, there's a parenting model that can guide your efforts—the model described and clarified in this book. Watch East Asian parents, learn from their approach to coaching and training their children, then go and do likewise.

If that's your choice, or if you'd like to at least take cautious steps in that direction, then consider making some or all of the following seven commitments to your child.

PARENTING WITH *GŬAN*:
SEVEN COMMITMENTS TO YOUR CHILD

In Discovery Step 8, we encountered the Chinese term *gŭan*. It's easy to pronounce: *gwahn*. *Gŭan* means "to be in charge of; to manage; to take care of, administer; to govern, control." *Gŭan* refers to the mindset and actions of a deeply caring, hands-on manager, not a coolly detached one. Applied to parenting, it means giving top priority to attentively guiding and molding your child's behavior, *partnering with* the child to guarantee that, academically (and perhaps in other ways), he or she will excel.

That top priority calls for a high degree of control, caretaking, participation, coaching, and training. It calls for *gŭan*. For a Chinese parent, *that's how love is demonstrated*.

Are you thinking of parenting with *gŭan*? Then here are seven commitments to make to your child.[6] Can't make them all at once? Begin by trying two or three, then adding more.

1. Your Exceptionality Will Be My Belief and Commitment

I will be your coach and trainer, dedicating myself to your attainment of *mastery* of academic skills. I will not view my role as facilitating your organic development. I will not treat you as though your mind is easily exhausted. I'll assume that you are malleable, resilient, and energetic, and that your brain is prepared to absorb much new information and tackle "stretch" challenges.

2. You'll Receive Direct Instruction from Me

I will directly guide and instruct you as you tackle ever more challenging tasks and concepts. In support of your dogged pursuit of mastery, I will drill you in basic skills and procedures. When appropriate, I will intervene to provide you with a model, to show you *how*, or to shape your actions. I won't shrink from the expert's role so long as I believe that I know more than you.

3. Your Use of Time Will Be Managed by Me

I will take charge of your waking hours to ensure that they are largely, if not entirely, devoted to the development of your academic skills and other skills that will set you apart from your peers. Your extracurricular pursuits will favor individual skill acquisition over social or team-focused activities. After finishing your homework each day, you'll continue studying toward mastery.

4. Your Outcomes Will Determine Your Self-Esteem

I will assume that your academic performance is due to your effort, not your inborn abilities. When you do extremely well, I'll praise your effort. When you don't, I'll expect more effort. Your self-esteem will rise and fall intrinsically—that is, in proportion to your attainment of goals. I will not try to inflate your self-esteem in cases when you haven't gained a successful outcome.

5. Your Failures Will Compel My Attention

I will take note of your successes, but I'll pay far more attention to your failures. I'll collaborate with you to figure out why you fell short. I'll participate side by side with you to ensure that you eventually master what you didn't know how to do. Our family will celebrate your overcoming of significant failures, and your mastery of academic tasks that you found especially challenging.

6. Your Learning Will Emphasize *How to Do* Things

I will ensure that you know *how to do* critical tasks. I'll show less concern for whether you can explain a task's principles, and more concern for whether you can accomplish its processes. I'll be pleased when you figure out *how to* on your own. Otherwise, I'll ensure that you learn *how to* by drilling you in fundamentals and/or providing you with my own, or others', direct instruction.

7. Your Learning Will Be Competence Centered, Not Child Centered

Your academic exceptionality will be a central goal of our family, and your responsibility to our family. I'll expect you to master academic subjects and related skills (e.g., music). Proficiency won't be good enough. I'll protect you from teachers who promise to "draw out students' unique abilities," "appeal to students' learning styles," "encourage creativity," and so forth. *Your* purpose for attending classes will be to raise your academic prowess to an exceptional level.

FURTHER READING

If you'd like more detail about the researchers' findings, or simply wish to know what inspired the contents of chapter 10, read the following entries in the annotated bibliography at www.thedrivetolearn.info.

- Abboud, Soo Kim, & Jane Kim (2006). *Top of the Class: How Asian Parents Raise High Achievers—and How You Can Too*.
- Boe, Erling E., et al. (2002). Student task persistence in the Third International Mathematics and Science Study.
- Chao, Ruth K. (1995). Chinese and European American cultural models of the self, reflected in mothers' childrearing beliefs.
- Chao, Ruth K., & Vivian Tseng (2002). Parenting in Asia.
- Chen, Chuansheng, & David H. Uttal (1988). Cultural values, parents' beliefs, and children's achievement in the United States and China.
- Chen, Chuansheng, et al. (1996). Academic achievement and motivation of Chinese students: A cross-national perspective.
- Cheng, Rebecca Wing-yi, et al. (2016). Motivation of Chinese learners: An integration of etic and emic approaches.
- Fong, Ricci W., & Man Tak Yuen (2016). The role of self-efficacy and connectedness in the academic success of Chinese learners.
- Fu, Alyssa S., & Hazel Rose Markus (2014). My mother and me: Why tiger mothers motivate Asian Americans but not European Americans.

- Hendry, Joy (1986). *Becoming Japanese: The World of the Pre-School Child.*
- Hess, Robert D., et al. (1986). Family influences on school readiness and achievement in Japan and the United States.
- Hess, Robert D., & Hiroshi Azuma (1991). Cultural support for schooling: Contrasts between Japan and the United States.
- Kao, Grace (1995). Asian Americans as model minorities? A look at their academic performance.
- Little, Todd D., et al. (2003). The links among action-control beliefs, intellective skill, and school performance in Japanese, U.S., and German school children.
- Mangels, Jennifer A., et al. (2006). Why do beliefs about intelligence influence learning success? A social cognitive neuroscience model. [Carol S. Dweck is a coauthor.]
- Park, Young-Shin, & Uichol Kim (2006). Family, parent-child relationship, and academic achievement in Korea: Indigenous cultural and psychological analysis.
- Parmar, Parminder, et al. (2008). Teacher or playmate? Asian immigrant and Euro-American parents' participation in their young children's daily activities.
- Pomerantz, Eva M., et al. (2011). Changes in early adolescents' sense of responsibility to parents in the United States and China: Implications for academic functioning.
- Schneider, Barbara, & Yongsook Lee (1990). A model for academic success: The school and home environment of East Asian students.
- Simons, Carol (1991). The education mother (*kyōiku mama*).
- Singleton, John (1989). *Gambaru*: A Japanese cultural theory of learning.
- Stevenson, Harold, & Shin-Ying Lee (1990). Contexts for achievement: A study of American, Chinese, and Japanese children.
- Stevenson, Harold W., & James W. Stigler (1992). *The Learning Gap: Why Our Schools Are Failing and What We Can Learn from Japanese and Chinese Education.*
- Wu, Peixia, et al. (2002). Similarities and differences in mothers' parenting of preschoolers in China and the United States.

Chapter Eleven

Responsibility and Creativity

Finally, two questions are worth further exploration. One is, "Who is responsible for a student's learning?" The other is, "Why are East Asians believed to be less creative than Americans?"

RESPONSIBILITY

Who Is Responsible for a Student's Learning?

An "ah-ha" moment in my career as an interculturalist came when I realized that the American value of self-determination did *not* necessarily mean that every individual takes responsibility for himself. The individual *may* take responsibility for himself. It's encouraged! But . . .

The main focus in the United States is on *individual rights*, also known as "freedom." We are more concerned about the freedom of a person to be, and to do, pretty much anything that does not infringe on anyone else's rights. Ideally, each individual will encounter few barriers to being and doing as he wishes. Others should take care to promote, and to avoid erecting barriers against, the individual's fulfillment. If they get in the individual's way, he may blame them or sue them. *Others are responsible for the individual.*

In East Asia, the focus is on the well-being of others, especially those in the most important groups to which the individual belongs (principally one's family, but also schoolmates, work team, etc.). Each group member looks out for the group's welfare. Each asks herself, "How will my behavior affect the other members?" and "What can I do to enhance my group's standing in the eyes of others?" If things go wrong, each member looks first at herself as a possible cause. *The individual is responsible for others.*

Responsibility for Learning in America

American schools spare no effort, within the limitations of their budget, to make themselves into places that children will want to attend. Many schools are physically attractive inside and out. Most have gymnasiums and cafeterias; some have swimming pools and sports arenas. Some have central heating and air conditioning. They offer an array of curricular electives and extracurricular activities. They are publicized as "child-centered" places where warm and friendly teachers try to make learning fun and—in order to promote each individual child's fulfillment—to accommodate their students' needs, preferences, styles, emerging interests, and capacity for self-expression.

We rarely expect children to gain more skill or knowledge than they must have to become "proficient." When many miss that modest mark, the adults usually lower the bar by means of grade inflation or a reduction of state-mandated standards. We don't want to discourage children, overly stress their brains, or damage their self-esteem. As Seiji, the child who attended school in the United States and Japan put it: In America, *"you [don't] really have to really, really do it."*[1]

What does all this tell us about the degree to which we believe our children are willing and able to take responsibility for their own learning? It's almost as though the gaining of knowledge is a stealth objective, a useful by-product of what some have ridiculed as "edutainment."

The findings of research completed between 1970 and the early 2000s strongly suggest that:

- After American children begin first grade, parents assume that the lion's share of responsibility for their learning is being handed to their teachers. For a variety of reasons, parents step back into the roles of protector, esteem-builder, and cheerleader—rarely that of coach or trainer.
- American children encounter few—if any!—situations in which the adults in their lives expect them to *master* academic skills or knowledge. Their learning bar is set at mere proficiency. If they attain that and show signs of becoming well liked and "well rounded," they're fine.
- Teachers shoulder most of the responsibility for students' learning. They provide an enjoyable learning situation, then facilitate the learning process while avoiding demands that might lead to student mental exhaustion. They're responsible for (a) presenting the material to be learned, (b) creating strategies that will enable the students to enjoy studying it, and will motivate them to want to study it, (c) evaluating how well each student has learned the material, and (d) providing opportunities for the students to express their uniqueness, such as making choices (which book to read, which term paper topic to choose) or expressing their opinions openly.

Responsibility for Learning in East Asia

In this book, I've said little about East Asian teachers, their teaching approaches, and their schools. We've deliberately concentrated on understanding East Asian students and their parents.

State-run schools in East Asia were pretty dismal places during the period when the research on which this book relies was completed. Most were unattractive, featuring large classrooms crammed with desks. There were few areas for play, no cafeterias, no pools or arenas, no intra- or intermural sports, and no electives. (Some offered extracurricular activities, but these were not necessarily school sponsored.) Edu-speak terms such as "child-centered" were not in vogue.[2]

For reasons that this book has explained, East Asian students arrived at these dismal schools with a drive to learn. Teachers centered their efforts on transmitting what was to be learned, feeling little need to accommodate the unique qualities of those being taught, and no need at all to make learning fun.[3] The students' gaining of knowledge wasn't a stealth objective; it was the *only* objective. And it was intertwined with the equally important, closely related objective of the students' learning to become virtuous human beings.

The findings of research completed between 1970 and the early 2000s strongly suggest that:

- After East Asian children begin school, parents assume that the lion's share of responsibility for their learning belongs to them and their child.[4] Parents embrace the role of coach.
- East Asian children often encounter situations in which the adults in their lives expect them to *master* academic skills or knowledge. At a minimum, they are expected to visibly persevere toward that goal. Their perseverance will make their families almost as proud as mastery will.
- Teachers shoulder *little* responsibility for students' learning. They master and expertly deliver the lessons, collaborating with fellow teachers to polish their delivery methods.[5] They do not need to provide enjoyable learning situations nor worry about student mental exhaustion. On the other hand, they *do* feel responsible for their students' overall development as exemplary human beings (which is not the same as American well-roundedness).[6]

Sample Observations from Researchers

Two researchers who studied American and Japanese elementary classrooms wrote that[7]

> U.S. teachers [appeared to believe] that students need to be prodded, enticed, and/or even threatened to study. Compared to the Japanese teachers, the U.S.

teachers seemed to assume more responsibility for helping students stay on task; they reminded them of time remaining, accountability, rewards, and so forth. They . . . frequently offered individual assistance when students needed help.

Japanese teachers . . . seemed to rely on intrinsic motivation to drive learning rather than extrinsic rewards or punishments. [They assumed] less responsibility for keeping children on task. Compared to the U.S. teachers, [they] used fewer time reminders and remarks to hurry students. They also tended to help individual students less frequently than the U.S. teachers did. No external reward system was observed.

Three researchers studied university faculty (including Westerners) and students in Hong Kong,[8] investigating who they believe is responsible for effective teaching. They wrote:

From a traditional Chinese perspective . . . , if I am a poor student, it is because I have not tried hard enough. [Some Chinese] students and faculty were in accord with traditional views [while others said] that effectiveness is a shared responsibility between teacher and learners. Rarely did [any Chinese respondent] suggest that effective teaching was solely attributable to the teacher.

The Western teachers in our study seldom attributed responsibility to the students alone, and most often accepted sole responsibility for whether or not they were effective teachers.

The American Perspective, Demonstrated

In August 2016, the "Commentary" section of *Education Week* featured an opinion piece[9] by a retired school superintendent who is on the faculty of a graduate school of education. The article's title was, "Who Should Be Responsible for Student Learning?" Noting the poor results of the latest National Assessment of Educational Progress, the author assesses state graduation standards, No Child Left Behind, the Common Core, teachers unions, charter schools, and teacher-related factors such as certification, accountability, and tenure. Family poverty gets a mention.

Not even imagined is the possibility that students could be responsible for their own learning.

A Difference in How Americans Assign Responsibility

A mystery of American schools has been why parents, students, and others behave in one way regarding academics, in another way regarding athletics. If we had asked, "Who is responsible for an *athlete's performance?*" we'd be discussing the athlete's responsibility to master basic skills via persistent drill and practice, to build strength and stamina, to learn from failure, and to benefit from the coaches' guidance. We'd note the passionate support of parents, students, and local residents.

Yes, a home run or touchdown pass is far more exhilarating than a young person's getting the top grade on a major examination. Well, here we go again: *That's true if you're an American*. If you're an East Asian, it's probably not true. Most East Asians are playing a different game.

Here is the likely reason why we Americans behave one way regarding academics and another way regarding athletics. We put athletics and academics into *different mental categories*:

- We view athletes as malleable, so that persevering hard work is likely to increase their athletic prowess. We believe they're highly resilient, have boundless energy, and are able to withstand constant drill and practice. For athletics, we prefer Carol Dweck's "growth mindset."
- We view young learners as constrained by their inborn aptitude. We think that persevering mental work could impair their delicate brains[10] *and* will bore and demotivate them. For academics, we apply Dweck's "fixed mindset," then ask, "So if efforts to upgrade one's academic ability will likely fail due to inborn aptitude, why expect a child to keep on trying?"

Who is responsible for a student's learning? In the United States, it's largely his teachers. In East Asia, it's largely the student—as her part of the collective responsibility she shares with her family.

How Some Children Learn Responsibility

We mustn't leave the topic of responsibility without hearing the conclusions of two researchers who revealed how children in communitarian societies learn responsibility.[11] It boils down to this: In the United States, we idealize egalitarian relations with our children, we view childhood as a time of self-motivated play, we give children endless choices, and we tolerate disobedience. In almost all communitarian societies, adults train and expect their children to be respectful and obedient, and to be accountable for the completion of one of the family's essential daily activities.

Even toddlers contribute, for example, by carrying small items from one adult to another. As they grow, toddlers are expected to watch, learn, and increasingly get involved. By the time they are age 6, they have genuine responsibilities: tasks vital to the family's welfare that they shoulder *without adult intervention*. Girls care for a younger sibling and help prepare food. Boys herd animals and help build houses. Some boys and girls have their own garden plots. Does this mean they never experience fun? Not at all. They find ways to have fun while being productive.

The researcher who gave us "Seiji" (see Discovery Step 9) compared Japanese and American responsibility training in schools. In Japan, pupils carried out duties on a regular basis, including serving lunch *and cleaning the entire school*. In Michigan, students also had duties, "but the schoolday did not depend on their successful execution."[12] That's the core meaning of responsibility: a duty that others expect *you* to do, so that if you don't, then *they* are inconvenienced or injured.

Amazingly, the research strongly suggests that children with a communitarian upbringing are more self-reliant than American children. Or maybe not amazing: After all, if at age 6 or 7 you're spending hours each day as the sole caretaker of your 2-year-old brother, as the lone shepherd of 30 or 40 goats, or as the harvester of the garden you planted in the spring, you're not only accountable for fulfilling an essential task. You are also entirely relying upon yourself.

CREATIVITY

Why are East Asians Believed to Be Less Creative than Americans?

If you mention to someone that East Asian students outperform American students, chances are that his quick reply will go something like, "Yeah, but our students are *way* more creative!" You might even hear about the chasm between our and their count of Nobel Prize winners.[13]

The creativity of youth was addressed in *World Class Learners: Educating Creative and Entrepreneurial Students*, a 2012 book by Professor Yong Zhao. Dr. Zhao's book isn't boasting that American students are more creative. Rather, its message is that, yes, American students are more creative, but their creativity is declining at this moment in history when far more creative entrepreneurship is needed by the American economy.

What's fascinating about Dr. Zhao's point of view is that he blames declining American creativity on American schools. The influence of culture barely gets a mention in his book. The influence of family is dismissed in a single sentence:[14]

> Schools are the primary institution for our children besides family, and therefore the primary place that shapes the experiences our children have.

That's it for families! In Dr. Zhao's index, neither "family" nor "culture" appears.[15]

Dr. Zhao's approach is a fine example of deductive reasoning. He begins with an axiom—a statement that *he accepts as self-evidently true*—the quoted sentence above. On that basis, he writes an entire book about certain ills of American schooling and how to fix them.

That's not how anthropologists do their jobs. They look at a situation and wonder, "What's going on here?"[16] Then they widely observe and participate, ponder how pieces of evidence might fit together, *and, finally, reach conclusions.* This approach is called inductive reasoning.

What Creativity Means in American and East Asian Cultures

Different meanings and values about creativity are being transmitted to children by families, schools, the media, and the culture at large in both the United States and East Asia. Here are five of the most easily observed contrasts.[17]

First, consider these meanings of creativity in the United States and East Asia. We're talking not only about the arts and humanities realm, but also about business, engineering, science, education, and the like.

- NOVELTY/ELABORATION: In the United States (and much of the West), what is regarded as creative or innovative is something that's new and different. We like "breakthroughs"; we admire the unique individuals who devise them. In East Asia (and Asia generally), what's regarded as creative or innovative is a subtle improvement of, or nuanced elaboration on, something that's traditional or at least familiar. The creative object or idea reveals the traditional in a new way. People admire something different if it's *slightly* different as well as socially useful.
- INSIGHTFUL/INCREMENTAL: Americans assume that an individual's fate depends heavily on his inborn aptitude or "gifts." This leads to our belief that a brilliant, creative idea is likely to come in a flash of insight, a genius's "ah-ha moment." East Asians assume that effort is more likely to yield results than aptitude, and that learning is a gradual, incremental process. Some scholars of creativity conclude that Americans are more interested in the "what" or "product" of the creation or innovation, while East Asians are more interested in the "how" or "process."
- AMORAL/MORAL: In the United States, artistic creativity outside of religious contexts is rarely associated with morality. Artistic creations may puncture the limits of what most people believe is proper; they should be "edgy." Artists are people who defy, or at least outpace, the crowd. In East Asia, artistic creativity should be guided by, and reflect, conventional morality. Admired artists are those who express the crowd, perhaps with slightly nuanced perspectives.

Also consider two differences in American and East Asian values and social expectations. Both were mentioned earlier in this book. Now we'll see how they support notions of creativity.

- DEBATE/DIALECTICS: In Discovery Step 7, "Thinking like a Historian," we discussed ways of life in ancient Greece. We noted the tradition of debate among individuals and in the formation of public policy [*dēmokratia*]. This led to today's Western style of thought,[18] which is oriented toward determining "right vs. wrong." In ancient East Asia, ways of life emphasized interdependence and cooperation, so a distinct pattern emerged. When people disagreed, their objective was to seek a resolution that branded neither position as wrong. Long known as "finding the middle way," this approach to thinking is also called "dialectical." Dialectical thought doesn't polarize or dichotomize; it doesn't reward uniqueness or seek breakthroughs.
- HIERARCHICAL/EGALITARIAN: East Asian traditions include the expectation that people will show respect and deference to those above them in the hierarchy. The ladder of hierarchy is climbed by one's gaining in age, and in knowledge and wisdom. Even today, schoolteachers are respected as masters because they are *the ones who know*. Specialists of all types are *the ones who know*. Learners do not try to quickly reveal their unique vision; rather, they use the technique of the one who knows as a model to be imitated. After years of gaining mastery, they may begin offering subtle departures from the established way. Americans' egalitarian, insight-admiring, uniqueness-seeking patterns of thought lead to very different outcomes.

Why Are East Asians Believed to Be Less Creative?

When it's we Americans and other Westerners who are judging what is admirably creative, you may be sure that the ones receiving prizes for their breakthrough products and unprecedented ideas will frequently be people raised in (or otherwise strongly influenced by) Western culture.

Let's wonder what path this discussion would be taking if, instead of the Nobel Prizes, the people of the world had the *Jiǎng Prizes*, conceived by an East Asian and awarded in Shanghai. How would the count of Western laureates compare with the count of East Asian laureates?

Yes, East Asians are less creative than American students—that is, when the world's peoples are judged by the Western values underlying, and meanings for, "creativity" and "innovation." Does this mean that we can feel good about our students' learning academic subjects poorly?

Remember this: Students' academic performance in the STEM subjects (science, technology, engineering, and mathematics) and reading is judged by standards that come quite close to being worldwide in application.[19] But creativity/innovation is being judged by standards that are distinctly Western. One of those playing fields is pretty near level. The other is sharply tilted.

If What You Want Is Western-Style Creativity . . .

Dr. Yong Zhao and others find *Western-style* creativity enticing. Among its admirers are plenty of educational policy makers in East Asia, especially in China, where major changes in educational policy and practice were announced in 1999.[20] Just like Dr. Zhao, those Chinese decision makers believed that a shortfall in (Western-style) creativity could be corrected by *schools*.

One anthropologist spent two years in Beijing exploring the ways in which the schools were attempting to upgrade creativity.[21] Her findings tell a story of failure, and for a variety of reasons. Interesting for us is the gap between the (Western) view of creativity that some Beijing teachers had adopted at the government's behest, and those same teachers' deep assumptions about creativity, which were consistent with Chinese cultural values. An art teacher asked, "After all, how can anyone be creative at art before they understand the fundamentals?" Echoed a music teacher, "They have to learn the scales first, before they can be creative about anything, right? How can [my students] raise their quality without a foundation first?"

No one denies that schools are influential in the lives of youth. But the argument that schools can make or break young people's capacity for creativity is flawed. *A school is the creature of the culture in which it exists.* A society erects and staffs schools not only to increase students' knowledge, but also to be a leading influence—second to families—in preparing students to participate in adult society and culture. Could a school, for most of its students, reverse behavior, meaning, and values deeply rooted within its containing culture? Believe it when you see it.

In short, if the wider culture containing a school has little fertile ground in which Western-style creativity can flourish, then whatever difference that school can make will be modest at best.

Why are East Asians believed to be less creative than Americans? Because we are applying *our* values and expectations about creativity as we judge *their* products of creative endeavor.

FURTHER READING

If you'd like more detail about the researchers' findings, or simply wish to know what inspired the contents of chapter 11, read the following entries in the annotated bibliography at www.thedrivetolearn.info.

About Responsibility

- Abboud, Soo Kim, & Jane Kim (2006). *Top of the Class: How Asian Parents Raise High Achievers—and How You Can Too.* [See especially chapter 17.]
- Damrow, Amy (2014). Navigating the structures of elementary school in the United States and Japan.
- Hess, Robert D., & Hiroshi Azuma (1991). Cultural support for schooling: Contrasts between Japan and the United States.
- Hsu, Francis L. K. (1981). *Americans & Chinese: Passage to Differences* (3rd ed.).
- Lewis, Catherine C. (1995). *Educating Hearts and Minds: Reflections on Japanese Preschool and Elementary Education.*
- Pomerantz, Eva M., et al. (2011). Changes in early adolescents' sense of responsibility to parents in the United States and China.
- Pratt, Daniel D., et al. (1999). Chinese conceptions of "effective teaching" in Hong Kong.
- Salili, Farideh (1996). Accepting personal responsibility for learning.
- Salzman, Mark (1986). *Iron & Silk.*
- Sato, Nancy, & Milbrey W. McLaughlin (1992). Context matters: Teaching in Japan and the United States.
- Stevenson, Harold W., & James W. Stigler (1992). *The Learning Gap: Why Our Schools Are Failing and What We Can Learn from Japanese and Chinese Education.*
- Tsuchida, Ineko, & Catherine C. Lewis (1998). Responsibility and learning: Some preliminary hypotheses about Japanese elementary classrooms.

About Creativity

- Cheng, Kai-ming (1998). Can education values be borrowed? Looking into cultural differences.
- Fryer, Marilyn, & Caroline Fryer-Bolingbroke (2011). Cross-cultural differences in creativity.
- Gardner, Howard (1989). *To Open Minds: Chinese Clues to the Dilemma of Contemporary Education.*
- Jin, Lixian, & Martin Cortazzi (2006). Changing practices in Chinese cultures of learning.
- Keller, Heidi (2003). Socialization for competence: Cultural models of infancy.
- Morris, Michael W., & Kwok Leung (2010). Editors' Forum: Creativity East and West.
- Niu, Weihua, & Robert J. Sternberg (2006). The philosophical roots of Western and Eastern conceptions of creativity.

Postscript

A few months before I finished writing *The Drive to Learn*, two books by acclaimed social scientists appeared within weeks of each other. One was by a developmental psychologist, the other by a husband-and-wife team of anthropologists. Both books—especially the one by the anthropologists—discuss some of the same issues that I've dealt with in this one.

The developmental psychologist is Alison Gopnik of the University of California at Berkeley. Gopnik's book is titled *The Gardner and the Carpenter: What the New Science of Child Development Tells Us about the Relationship between Parents and Children*.

The anthropologists are Robert A. LeVine of Harvard University, and his wife Sarah LeVine. Their book is titled *Do Parents Matter? Why Japanese Babies Sleep Soundly, Mexican Siblings Don't Fight, and American Families Should Just Relax*.

The message of both books? The final phrase in the LeVines's subtitle sums up what they and Gopnik are saying to American parents: *Just relax!* Stop worrying and striving and exhausting yourselves (*and* your children) trying to fine-tune your "parenting" so perfectly that, when your children become adults, they're guaranteed to lead satisfying, productive lives.

The View of an Eminent Developmental Psychologist

Alison Gopnik doesn't like the word "parent" used as a verb: to parent.[1] The verb form, she says, makes parenting into a kind of work, the goal of which "is to somehow turn your child into a better or happier or more successful adult—better than they would be otherwise." Many of the 60,000+ books in the parenting section of Amazon, she notes, promise that the right parenting techniques can make a big difference in the way a child turns out. She tells the reader that she's going to "argue that this prescriptive parenting picture is fundamentally misguided."

Gopnik's title mentions a "carpenter" and a "gardener." A carpenter, notes Gopnik, is a person who sets out to build something with a definite final form in view, to be realized through the use of specific tools and techniques. This she likens to the verb form of "parent," and that's what she hopes to persuade Americans with children to *stop* doing.

A gardener, on the other hand, is a person who sets out to nurture and support something that's able to grow and flower largely on its own. Gopnik is eloquent on this point:[2]

> Love doesn't have goals or benchmarks or blueprints, but it does have a purpose. The purpose is not to change the people we love, but to give them what they need to thrive. Love's purpose is not to shape our beloved's destiny, but to help them shape their own. Loving children doesn't give them a destination; it gives them sustenance for the journey.

Perhaps you find this passage warmly appealing. I do! But let's ask whether the emotion aroused by Gopnik's eloquence is not about you and me, but rather about the American culture we share. You, Alison Gopnik, and I, as people shaped by our individualistic culture (explained in Discovery Step 6), are programmed to find this way of thinking warmly appealing. Where did our programming come from? The answer takes us deeply into Western history, as revealed in my 2013 book, *The Aptitude Myth*.

Gopnik counsels us to return to the gardener's way. She urges parents to abandon the use of parenting techniques devised by "experts" in the belief that they will produce adult children with satisfying, productive lives. How did we come to rely on experts' parenting advice?

During the 1970s, Gopnik explains, families started becoming mobile.[3] Young parents increasingly resided far from grandparents and other senior family members. Traditional wisdom largely disappeared from the daily life of parents and children. In their stead came how-to books, women's magazines, speakers, websites, and social media. Middle-class parents, accustomed to learning in schools and colleges from experts (teachers and professors) in pursuit of long-term goals such as a career, applied the expert model to help them figure out how to be good parents.

For a more detailed answer to the question of where belief in the carpenter's way of parenting came from, we need to turn to *Do Parents Matter?* by Robert and Sarah LeVine.

The View of Two Eminent Anthropologists of Childhood

A useful feature of *Do Parents Matter?* is its history of the origins of what Gopnik calls "the carpenter's way" and the LeVines call "the psychiatric perspective." In their first chapter, "Parent-Blaming in America," the LeVines tell the story of experts in public health, pediatrics, and psychiatry who, since the late 19th century, have "claimed the authority of science while blending moral ideology with (incomplete) empirical evidence."[4] In the rogues' gallery of experts whom they dissect, the worst offender is Bruno Bettleheim, who "liked to confront mothers with what he regarded as their sins."[5] The LeVines brand his and others' advice as "unscientific."

The most useful feature of the LeVines's book is its broad, detailed perspective on parenting and child development in a variety of cultures. The LeVines cover some of the same ground that I have, especially in Discovery Step 6. Echoing Gopnik, they call on parents to abandon the dual notions that (a) *if they don't* do everything right, they'll drive their child into mental illness; but (b) *if they do* do everything right, they'll virtually guarantee that their child will enjoy a successful, fulfilling adulthood.[6] Here is the LeVines's own conclusion:[7]

> As we have seen, the influence of parenting on child development has been grossly exaggerated in the mass media, which inflates its predictability beyond the evidence and underestimates the resilience of children and the likelihood of change in later childhood and adolescence. The time has come for American parents to reconsider the burdens they place on themselves for dubious ends.

DOES MY ADVICE CONTRADICT THEIRS?

The LeVines counsel, "Just relax!" Gopnik urges, "Become a gardener." Their appeals sound sharply different from the "Seven Commitments to Your Child" that I suggest in chapter 10.

On the surface, these approaches to child-rearing seem contradictory. But as you've witnessed again and again in this book, when you devote time and effort to inquiring deeply, you begin to appreciate that *in human affairs, surface appearances often distort what's really going on.*

Both Gopnik and the LeVines address American parenting—in particular American middle-class parenting—in exceptionally broad terms. Both books are on a mission to get parents to stop trying to guarantee that their children will avoid mental illness and grow up to enjoy satisfying and fruitful adult lives. Both books say, "That's not possible, so stop trying."

It was never my mission to reform American parenting. Instead, I joined the decades-long chorus of concern over our children's poor performance in school, compared with children in several other developed societies. In pursuit of solutions, reformers have investigated and criticized every educator-influenced aspect of schooling. I do something completely different: I examine the children's role in poor performance. From their first day in school, our children demonstrate relatively low receptivity to school learning. *The solution for that lies with parents.*

The Drive to Learn deals with one narrow issue, poor school performance. It finds that children are part of the problem . . . and therefore must be part of the solution. *For those parents who are eager for their children to excel in school*, a solution is offered based on what we know about East Asian child-training. In this book, I sidestep the question of whether top students' adult lives will be exemplary.[8] I'm focused solely on their classroom performance.

Gopnik notes that "schooling requires the ability to focus attention narrowly,"[9] but offers no suggestions about how parents can foster that. The LeVines devote three pages to how Chinese parents foster their children's school learning. They quote Jin Li (see Discovery Step 4) and finally exclaim, "No wonder the children of Chinese immigrants do well in school here in North America!"[10] So, no, my advice does not contradict that of Gopnik or the LeVines.

But wait! Isn't there a more subtle conflict? Aren't Gopnik and the LeVines saying that, actually, parents have far less influence over their children's lives than the experts like to claim?

That's not what Gopnik and the LeVines are saying. With respect to *very young children*, the influence of parents (or other major caregivers) overwhelms that from any other source. The point that Gopnik and the LeVines make is that, as the child grows, other factors come into play ever more strongly: playmates, teachers, kinfolk and family friends, illnesses and injuries, dramatic experiences. . . . Some inevitably become significantly more influential in shaping the child's adult life than the parental factor. That's why parents should just relax and garden!

But in this book, I'm not dealing with any of that. I'm dealing with a single problem of great importance to many Americans: children's poor school performance. I am saying that the solution does not lie entirely with educator-controlled practices and policies. A major part of the solution lies with the children—with very young children. Therefore, a major part lies with their parents.

Notes

PREFACE

1. See Grove (1977).
2. See Hu & Grove (1999). The third edition, with a new subtitle and a third coauthor, was published in 2010. See Hu, Grove, & Enping (2010).
3. See Grove (2006) [annotated]. Available to read in full by searching the web for pub-instructional-styles.
4. The *Encyclopedia of Intercultural Competence* was published in 2015. The *International Encyclopedia of Intercultural Communication* is on course to be published during 2018.
5. Aka, Baka, Hadza, !Kung, Pirahã, Qashqa'i, Sámi, Yanomamö, and Tapirapé. These are just a few of the 450 societies listed in the "Society Index" in Lancy (2015) [annotated].

INTRODUCTION

1. Respected educational historian and researcher Diane Ravitch (2014) has argued that we need not be concerned about American students' repeated mediocre performances on the international comparative tests. For example, she has written, "Let [other nations] have the higher test scores. I prefer to bet on the creative, can-do spirit of the American people, on its character, persistence, ambition, hard work, and big dreams, none of which are ever measured or can be measured by standardized tests like PISA."

On the other hand, you might also want to take into account reports such as one that appeared in the *New York Times* on December 27, 2015 (p. A1), titled "As Graduation Rates Rise, a Fear [That] Diplomas Fall Short"; and its associated editorial on December 31, 2015 (p. A22), titled "The Counterfeit High School Diploma." The

118   Notes

latter summarizes that "[l]ess than 40 percent of 12th graders are ready for math and reading at the college level."

2. As an example, consider Pasi Sahlberg's *Finnish Lessons 2.0* (2015). This book is almost entirely about the procedures and policies of adult educators and educational policy makers in Finland. A section titled "Student Learning" (pp. 68–80) is about statistical measures and includes four charts. The index does not include the terms "student," "children," "family," "home," "parenting," or "child-rearing"; the term "family background" in the index references socioeconomic factors. On page 86, one sentence discusses the admirable Finnish cultural value *sisu*, "strength of will." In sharp contrast, the book you're now reading includes extended discussions about cultural traits and values such as *gŭan* and *hào xúe xīn* in China, and *sunao* and *gambaru* in Japan.

3. Not every researcher cited herein would think of himself or herself as, specifically, an anthropologist. I'm using the term "anthropologist" broadly to designate researchers who primarily use their five senses to observe (including, sometimes, to count) the behavior patterns of teachers, students, parents, and children; who consider all that they observe within the context of the local community's shared values; and who inductively derive for each cultural group its prevailing assumptions about the goals and practices of child development and learning. This distinguishes these researchers from others, such as psychologists, who try to "get inside the heads" of individuals to reveal each one's cognitive abilities and preferences.

4. To make this book's message understandable, easily remembered, and applicable, in some cases I will weave whole cloth out of strands of research that the researchers themselves haven't linked together. I will connect some isolated dots to sketch a more recognizable image.

5. The most obvious difference is the manner in which Chinese and Japanese mothers attempt to inculcate in their children compliance with the expectations of adults. Japanese mothers' top priority is to protect the growing emotional bond (sometimes called a "sticky relationship") between mother and child; they virtually never scold or confront their child, preferring instead to preserve an intense closeness that builds the child's capacity for empathy. Chinese mothers' top priority is to ensure that the child learns proper behavior and moral virtue; they frequently confront their children, taking advantage of a misdeed (or even a remembered misdeed) to deliver what some would call "moral lectures" stressing desirable attitudes and behavior. See, for example, LeVine & LeVine (2016, pp. xvi–xvii).

6. For an analysis of China's "Education for Quality" policy, see Lin (2010).

CHAPTER 1

1. Facts about the First International Mathematics Study and the First International Science Study were taken from Ravitch (2014).

2. The nations whose 13-year-olds were ahead of ours were (from the top) Israel, Japan, Belgium, Finland, Germany, England, Scotland, The Netherlands, France, and

Australia. The Israelis' mean score was 32.3; the Americans' mean score was 17.8 (Medrich & Griffith, 1992, table B1, p. 67).

3. The entire text of *A Nation at Risk* is available online at the U.S. Department of Education archives.

4. Two books that grew out of this research were *The Shopping Mall High School: Winners and Losers in the Educational Marketplace* (1985), and *The Failed Promise of the American High School, 1890–1995* (1999). These books and other publications called attention to the lowering of the academic standards students were expected to attain, and the growing efforts to keep students engaged by offering them a wide variety of interesting, nondemanding options (hence, "the shopping mall school").

5. At www.NationsReportCard.gov is a one-screen "Nation's Report Card" that reveals the percentage of students who, on recent tests, performed "at or above proficient." (Note the emphasis on American students achieving "proficiency." Mastery is no longer the goal.)

6. TIMSS stands for Trends in International Mathematics and Science Studying. PISA means Program for International Student Assessment. Tables and other data from these tests are available at the international section of the website of the National Center for Education Statistics. For an engaging background look at the development of the PISA, see chapter 1, "The Treasure Map," in Amanda Ripley's 2013 book, *The Smartest Kids in the World: And How They Got That Way* [annotated].

7. The approach described is the one known as both "progressive" and "child centered." The description is based on an explanation found on the website Education.com.

CHAPTER 2

1. Biggs (1996b, pp. 46–47) [annotated]. Biggs credits K. Samuelowicz (1987, pp. 121–134).

2. Biggs (1996b, p. 47) [annotated]. Biggs credits D. Murphy (1987, pp. 43–44).

3. Cortazzi & Jin (2001, p. 125) [annotated]. The article offers no information about the quoted 8-year-old child except that he was Chinese.

4. Among the many criticisms of American education is that, in comparison with many other national systems, people need not have mastered their subject matter in order to be qualified to teach.

5. The amount of homework expected of American students is declining due in part to organized opposition to it. Visit www.stophomework.com and the more influential www.racetonowhere.com. Among the books criticizing homework is Etta Kralovec and John Buell's *The End of Homework: How Homework Disrupts Families, Overburdens Children, and Limits Learning* (2001).

6. For more details, see Tang (1996) [annotated].

7. For a more extensive discussion, see Li (2012, pp. 75, 138) [annotated].

8. Ference Marton et al. (1996, p. 81) [annotated]. The concept "memorization with understanding" is known among some educators as "internalization from practice" (personal communication, Young Mi Park).

9. The historical development of the belief in the powers of intuition and insight is traced in my 2013 book, *The Aptitude Myth: How an Ancient Belief Came to Undermine Children's Learning Today*.

CHAPTER 3

1. Professor Leonard Sayles of Columbia University's Graduate School of Business is the author of well-received books on management and leadership such as *Leadership: Managing in Real Organizations* (1989), *The Working Leader* (1993), and *The Rise of the Rogue Executive* (2005).
2. One reviewer wrote that "[p]rincipals can choose a stunt level that they are comfortable with and go from there."
3. A similar point about experts is made by psychologist Angela Duckworth in her 2016 book *Grit: The Power of Passion and Perseverance*. "[E]xperts are more interested in what they did wrong—so they can fix it—than what they did right" (p. 122; italics in original).
4. If you're curious about why Americans believe their children are born with fixed abilities, have a look at my book, *The Aptitude Myth: How an Ancient Belief Came to Undermine Children's Learning Today* (Grove, 2013).
5. Dweck was at Teachers College, Columbia University, when she and colleagues began this research. Of Dweck's publications, some with coauthors (including Asian coauthors), her best known is *Mindset: The New Psychology of Success* (2006). In the annotated bibliography, see Mangels et al. (2006); Dweck is a coauthor.
6. The distinction between American students' "performance goals" and East Asian students' "mastery goals" was drawn by Rebecca Wing-yi Cheng et al. (2016) [annotated].
7. The distinction between "self-improvement" and "self-enhancement" was drawn by Heine et al. (2001) [annotated].
8. There's a twist to how Americans react to high and low performance by students. How much a student studies isn't the only thing taken into account. Inborn ability also is very important.

- If a low-performing student is assumed to have high inborn ability, Americans blame him. They push him to work harder and "live up to his potential."
- If a low-performing student is assumed to have low inborn ability, Americans don't blame him. They view him as the victim of bad luck.
- If a high-performing student is assumed to have high inborn ability, Americans don't resent him. They view him as the beneficiary of good luck.
- If a high-performing student is assumed to have low inborn ability, Americans don't resent him. They admire that he's worked hard to overcome his bad luck.

However, among middle- and high-school peers, a student who is seen to work hard might be harassed or bullied. His peers might be assuming that he's gaining unfair advantage on exams or "sucking up" to authority. So here's a bit of advice for high school students: If you want your peers to think that you lucked out at birth, follow three rules: (a) definitely ace those tests; (b) don't study very hard; (c) if you *must* study hard, do it in secret!

The above analysis is based on two sources: Salili (1996, p. 92–95) [annotated]; and Li (2012, see especially the section titled "The Western Learner in the Eye of the Beholder") [annotated].

CHAPTER 4

1. Personal communication with Jin Li, May 17, 2016. For more about the "barefoot doctors," see National Public Radio (2005).
2. Li (2012, excerpts from p. 2 and note 4) [annotated].
3. Li (2012, pp. 3–4).
4. Li (2012, p. 6 [excerpted]).
5. Li (2012, excerpts pp. 8–9). Italics added.
6. Li (2012, excerpts pp. 12–13). Additional maxims are quoted there.
7. Li (2012, pp. 13–14).
8. Following is a more complete description of the process Jin Li used to obtain the two "initial lists" and the two "core lists":

   A. She determined that the words to explore would be "learn/learning" in English, and "*xúexí*" in Chinese.
   B. She asked three university students in each nation to write down all the words and phrases that came to their minds when they read (for the Americans) "learn/learning," and (for the Chinese) "*xúexí.*"
   C. She gave the *xúexí* list to another group of 20 Chinese students, and the learn/learning list to another group of 20 American students, asking for even more words and phrases; the resulting lists included 496 items for learn/learning and 478 items for *xúexí*. However, each of these two "initial lists" included items that Jin judged to be only weakly associated with learning.
   D. Jin gave the "initial lists" to a third group of 60 students in each nation, asking them to rate how strongly each word or phrase was related to learning.
   E. After she dropped all items that the students judged as weakly related to learning, the resulting "core lists" numbered 225 items for *xúexí*, and 203 items for learn/learning (Li, 2012, pp. 77–79).

9. Figure 4.1 is closely based on table 3.2 in Li (2012, p. 81).
10. Figure 4.2 reproduces the first 18 items (except for Chinese characters) found in table 3.1 in Li (2012, p. 80).
11. Dr. Li's model was not expressed as questions. The questions are my restatement of her (a) Purpose of Learning, (b) Agentic Process of Learning, (c) Kinds of Achievement, and (d) Affect, Positive and Negative. See Li (2012, pp. 85–97, especially table 3.3, page 86; additional elaboration is in the following chapter, pp. 105–147).

12. Dr. Li did not explain her findings via imaginary students. This is my device to enable readers to more readily grasp key elements of Dr. Li's findings, which are richer and far more extensively analyzed and discussed than my overview in the text suggests.

The words I put in the mouths of Andrew and Chunli are guided by, but not identical to, the words written by Dr. Li in her reports of her research findings. In some cases, I have departed somewhat from Dr. Li's findings in order to emphasize themes about East Asians being developed in this book. I have done this under the guidance of my advisers, who are experts in the Chinese and Japanese cultures: Kay M. Jones and Anthony Pan.

13. What is the purpose of learning? This section summarizes Dr. Li's discussion of purpose as found in Li (2012, pp. 85–86, 90–91). See also van Egmond et al. (2013, p. 210) [annotated]. This thoughtful article is grounded in Dr. Li's research, and Dr. Li is a coauthor.

14. How does one get learning done? This section summarizes Dr. Li's discussion of agentic process as found in Li (2012, pp. 87, 91–93, 90–91, 110–119, 123–147). See also van Egmond et al. (2013, p. 210–212), which is an extensive analysis of the American mind-oriented and process-oriented approach.

15. The limiting and constraining function of "potential" in American thinking about children's development is one of the principal themes of my 2013 book, *The Aptitude Myth*, where it is approached historically and with special attention to the influence of 19th-century English philosopher Herbert Spencer. Also, note that the work of contemporary American psychologist Carol S. Dweck resonates with the idea that, in the United States, "potential" is a limiting and constraining concept. See, within step 3 ("Exploring Motivations"), the discussion of Dweck's valuable findings regarding "fixed" and "growth" mindsets.

16. See Li (2004) [annotated]. Little Bear was liked by 96% of the Americans, but by merely 41% of the Chinese, whose disapproval of her learning behavior, which they viewed as flawed, undermined their attraction to her.

17. What outcomes does learning bring? This section summarizes Dr. Li's discussion of kinds of achievement as found in Li (2012, pp. 88 and 93).

18. What emotions are associated with learning? This section summarizes Dr. Li's discussion of affect as found in Li (2012, pp. 88–89 and 94–96). See also Li (2003), especially her "Discussion," pp. 264–266 [annotated].

19. Doubts about the applicability of "intrinsic" and "extrinsic" in East Asia were expressed as early as 1991 by Robert Hess and Hiroshi Azuma in their article "Cultural Support for Schooling: Contrasts between Japan and the United States" (1991) [annotated]. In 1996, concern was voiced by John Biggs in his article "Learning, Schooling, and Socialization: A Chinese Solution to a Western Problem" (1996a) [annotated]. Other researchers have come to agree that "intrinsic" and "extrinsic," terms developed by American psychologists, are not useful in understanding or describing East Asian students' determination to learn.

CHAPTER 5

1. This billboard, looking down on the corner of Third Avenue and President Street in Brooklyn, featured "Jonny Lavine | Polo Player" and was placed by the U.S. Polo Association.

2. Quoted is an excerpt from the first paragraph of a discussion of "Live Authentically," found on the website HowToLive.com. The owner of this website, Tom Murcko, describes himself as "an entrepreneur, connoisseur, and raconteur." Also available on this website are Mr. Murcko's discussions of, among many others, "Get motivated," "Find your why," "High self-esteem is essential for a well-lived life," and "Don't worry about what others think of you."

3. Quanyu Huang offers this explanation in his 2014 book, *The Hybrid Tiger* [annotated]. He notes that the written characters for Chinese pronouns—"you," "he," and such—all have a visible relationship to "people": The two brush strokes on the left side mean "people." But the character for *wŏ* lacks those strokes, suggesting that it's not about people. He explains that "traditional Chinese culture thought the self was equal to privacy and selfishness, two very negative characteristics devoid of virtue [and] the root of all evil. [So Chinese culture] wisely separated the self and the social role, then belittled the self and praised the social role" (2014, pp. 177–178).

4. Takie Sugiyama Lebra (1994) [annotated]. Dr. Lebra was a professor at the University of Hawai'i for many years. She is a respected, widely published authority on Japanese culture. See, for example, her 1976 book, *Japanese Patterns of Behavior*, or her 2004 book, *The Japanese Self in Cultural Logic*. Dr. Lebra once memorably described the Japanese self as "a fraction" of his or her family group.

5. The two diagrams and the commentary about them are from the article by Uichol Kim & Soo-Hyang Choi (1994, pp. 232–237 and figures 11.1 and 11.2) [annotated]. The quotes within the description of the left-hand diagram are attributed to Spence (1985, p. 1288).

6. See Iyengar & Mark R. Lepper (1999) [annotated]. The account in the text is a greatly simplified and shortened version of their 16-page journal article, which is considered a landmark study and is frequently cited by other scholars. For another research study that reached a similar but not identical conclusion, see Hamedani et al. (2013, 189–196).

7. Iyengar & Lepper used the terms "Asian American" and "Anglo American." The former were described thus: "The Asian American sample included only children who spoke their respective Asian languages of Japanese or Chinese at home with their parents, to increase the likelihood that these Asian American children were not already totally assimilated into American culture." The "Anglo American" pupils were not described. I have changed "Anglo American" to "Americans of European descent" (hereafter simply "Americans") to remove any suggestion that all these pupils were of British heritage. See Iyengar & Lepper (1999, p. 351).

8. Figure 5.3 closely reproduces figure 1 in Iyengar and Lepper (1999, p. 353). These findings were found to be statistically significant at an exceptionally high level: $p < .0001$ (less than one chance in 10,000). See page 352.

9. My version of what the researcher said to each child closely parallels, but does not exactly duplicate, the researcher's statements as quoted in Iyengar & Lepper (1999, pp. 351–352).

10. Figure 5.4 closely reproduces figure 2 in Iyengar & Lepper (1999, p. 354). These findings were found to be statistically significant at an exceptionally high level: $p < .0001$ (less than one chance in 10,000). See page 353.

11. My cultural advisers for East Asia, Kay M. Jones and Anthony Pan, prompted me to add that an East Asian child's feeling of unity would be combined with feelings of respect and loyalty toward her mother. They pointed out that "the parent/child relationship is one of the Confucian five 'cardinal' hierarchical relationships. Those on top are supposed to demonstrate competence and caring. Those below are supposed to show loyalty and respect. The teacher/student relationship is modeled after parent/child." They go on to hypothesize that if the directives to subgroup C had come from the child's teacher ("Teacher's Choice"), the outcome—the child's outstanding performance—would have been similar.

12. A recent study has uncovered errors in fMRI software that can cause false positives (brain activity is reported when actually there is none) up to 70% of the time. This revelation potentially calls into question the findings reported here, plus thousands of others. I have retained this section in the text because the findings of Zhu et al. (2007) confirm what anthropologists and others have long expected on the basis of completely different research methods. See Eklund et al. (2016). See also Murphy (2016).

13. Zhu et al. (2007) [annotated]. The account in the text is a greatly simplified and shortened version of their seven-page journal article, which was one of the first to examine neurological events in the mPFC with respect to representation of self and mother.

14. Figure 5.5 closely reproduces figure 4c in Zhu et al. (2007, p. 1315), which is discussed in the text on pp. 1312–1313. However, the precise percentage figures are not provided in either the text or the figure. Figure 5.5 comes as close as my naked eye can gauge, based on figure 4c in Zhu et al. (2007).

Another difference was found as well. When the Chinese students made judgments about their mothers, two other areas of their brains also had an increase in activity: the left prefrontal cortex and the anterior cingulate cortex. The Western students showed no such changes. See figure 4d in Zhu et al. (2007, p. 1315), which is discussed in the text pp. 1312–1313.

15. Other studies using the same technology have reached similar findings. Here are six that you might wish to explore with the aid of Google Scholar [none is included in the annotated bibliography]:

- Chen, Pin-Hao A., et al. (2013). Medial prefrontal cortex differentiates self from mother in Chinese: Evidence from self-motivated immigrants. *Culture and Brain, 1*(1), 3–15.
- Chiao, Joan Y., et al. (2009). Neural basis of individualistic and collectivistic views of self. *Human Brain Mapping, 30*(9), 2813–2820.

- Chiao, Joan Y., et al. (2010). Dynamic cultural influences on neural representations of the self. *Journal of Cognitive Neuroscience, 22*(1), 1–11.
- Han, Shihui, & Glyn Humphreys. (2016). Self-construal: A cultural framework for brain function. *Current Opinion in Psychology, 8*, 10–14. [This is a review of recent research.]
- Han, Shihui, & Georg Northoff. (2009). Understanding the self: A cultural neuroscience approach. *Progress in Brain Research, 178*, 203–212.
- Li, Zhang et al. (2006). In search of the Chinese self: An fMRI study. *Science in China, Series C, 49*(1), 89–96.

16. Duckworth (2016, pp. 143–146).

17. Junger (2016, p. 52). Junger discusses the fact that when people living in modern Western (individualistic) societies have an extended experience of tribal (communitarian) living, they prefer it.

18. *Hào* [fourth tone] is a verb that means "to love" or "to desire." (Do not confuse it with *hǎo* [third tone], meaning "good" or "well.") *Xúe* is a noun that means knowledge, learning, or studying. *Xīn* means "heart"; in the traditional Chinese mindset, feelings, emotions, and thoughts come from the heart. Literally, *hào xúe xīn* means "love learning heart." Dr. Li's translation, "heart and mind for wanting to learn," combines the concept of heart from the Chinese perspective with the concept of mind from the Western perspective [KJ & AP].

CHAPTER 6

1. Gardner (1989, pp. 3–4, 5) [annotated].

2. The overviews of the two types of societies rely largely on Heidi Keller (2003, pp. 289–292) [annotated]. Keller uses the standard sociological names for these two society types: "industrialized" and "traditional." Given the current high levels of industrialization and urbanization in East Asia, I have substituted "individualized" and "communitarian."

Also taken into consideration are the views of David F. Lancy (2015) [annotated]. As reported in Discovery Step 6, Lancy notes that the ethnographic and historical records show that, in order to become competent within their cultures, children do not need formal schooling. Classroom instruction arose, says Lancy, due to the growing complexity of societies (which required learned administrators), the increasing specialization of craftsmen, and—eventually—"knowledge workers."

3. Still other names include "information" and "European." In addition, these societies have been branded as WEIRD—Western, Educated, Industrialized, Rich, and Democratic. Up until the end of the 20th century, virtually all research on human beings was carried out on subjects and groups in WEIRD societies. David Lancy makes two points in his essay titled "The Anthropologist's Veto" (2015, pp. 1–4): First, WEIRD people are the worst possible subjects if one wants to understand *Homo sapiens* because they are highly unrepresentative of the entire human race throughout history. Second, to make matters worse, most research subjects have been college

undergraduates, and many of them were Americans attending colleges in their native America!

The unrepresentativeness of WEIRD societies was first noted by Henrich et al. (2010).

4. This account relies heavily on Keller (2003, pp. 301–306). Her subhead for this section of her research report is "The Infant as (Quasi) Equal Partner in Social Communication."

5. The long-range objective of the parents was that the child become self-reliant, thus needing to depend less and less on them. Keller summarizes by writing that the infant's early experiences "establish a separate agency in the infant which enables him or her to explore the physical and social world independently." Keller (2003, p. 304). "Agency" is a term in sociology and philosophy referring to a person's capacity to act in the environment in a way that attains, or could attain, an objective of some kind.

6. This account relies heavily on Keller (2003, pp. 294–301). Her subhead for this section of her paper is "The Expert-Novice Relationship of Parenting."

7. Nso mothers frequently lift their baby up and down, sometimes holding only its hands, and stretch the baby's legs. These are not casual activities, but ones for which there are widely shared, explicit criteria. For example, lifting is appropriate only after six months, is inappropriate right after breastfeeding, should not be too vehement, and should not include supporting the baby's head. Mothers believe that stimulation accelerates the baby's gross motor development. When shown videotapes of German mothers leaving their babies lying on their backs, the Nso mothers were strongly critical, claiming that the infant's development would be retarded. Keller (2003, p. 298).

8. This account relies on Correa-Chávez & Rogoff (2009). The Mayan children all had mothers with six or fewer years of schooling, averaging only two grades. Their fathers averaged five grades of schooling; the majority worked as day laborers. The American children all had mothers with at least 12 years of schooling, averaging 16 grades [college graduation]. Their fathers also averaged 16 grades; all were employed in business or the professions. The account in the text is a greatly simplified version of the research report by Correa-Chávez & Rogoff; for example, there was a third group of subjects and a second toy to be assembled. Dr. Barbara Rogoff, of the University of California at Santa Cruz, has long been a leading figure in studying how children learn; her research has focused on indigenous communities in the Americas.

9. Coding of the nonparticipating sibling's behavior occurred in 5-second segments. The Mayan siblings paid sustained attention in 62.4% of the segments while the American siblings did so in only 30.6% of the segments; this difference was significant ($p < .01$). The American siblings paid no attention in 48.6% and gave brief glances in 22.6% of the segments, but the Mayan siblings paid no attention in 33.2% and gave brief glances in only 4.4% of the segments; these differences also were significant ($p < .01$). Correa-Chávez & Rogoff (2009, pp. 635–636 and table 2).

10. What was coded was the amount of assistance needed to assemble the frog 10 days later. The older Mayan siblings received assistance in 43.5% of the segments while the older American siblings received assistance in 58.8% of the segments; this

difference was significant (p < .01). Across both cultural backgrounds, children who engaged in more sustained attention needed less assistance ten days later; this difference was significant (p < .01). Correa-Chávez & Rogoff (2009, pp. 637–638 and table 3).

11. The quote unites sentences in three adjacent paragraphs in Correa-Chávez & Rogoff (2009, pp. 630–631). The quote about Navajo children is attributed to Collier Jr. (1988, p. 262). In the next paragraph, Correa-Chávez and Rogoff write:

> Restrictions on opportunities to observe may relate to the frequent engagement of middle-class adults in managing children's attention and learning in child-focused conversations and mini-lessons. For example, when showing toddlers how to operate novel toys, middle-class caregivers . . . often provide children with language lessons and use mock excitement and praise to manage the children's attention and involvement. Similarly, . . . mothers in a teaching situation took responsibility for making their toddlers learn by trying to arouse interest and refocus attention, whereas Gusii (Kenyan) mothers with little schooling seemed to expect toddlers to be able to take responsibility for completing the task as shown.

12. The first six pages of Heidi Keller's article review research literature about child-rearing in different types of society. See also her five-page bibliography. Keller (2003, pp. 288–311). And the first three pages of Correa-Chávez and Rogoff's article review research literature focused on children's observation and attention (2009, pp. 630–641). For an even more comprehensive perspective, see LeVine & LeVine (2016), especially chapter 4, "Mother and Infant: Face-to-Face or Skin-to-Skin."

13. Keller (2003, p. 300). Later in this paragraph, Keller writes:

> Children participate in sociocultural activities by imitation and guided participation. Yet it is not merely the joint activity . . . but also explicit cultural teaching, mainly by older siblings. Children from [as] early as three years of life monitor their younger siblings' activities and teach them everyday tasks. The close relationship between the siblings as well as the emphasis on obedience from the younger to the older helps children develop valued social skills.

14. Gardner (1989, p. 5).
15. Gardner (1989, p. 5).

CHAPTER 7

1. Lancy (2015, pp. 327–328) [annotated]. Later in that paragraph, Lancy adds: "The central theme of [chapter 7, "Taming the Autonomous Learner"] is the 'strangeness' of the modern practice of schooling. I use the term 'strange' because, in a survey of childhood across history and culture, the suite of practices and teaching/learning abilities associated with modern schooling is largely absent."

2. Kramer (1963, pp. 238–239); quoted in Lancy (2015, p. 330). Lancy footnotes the word "caned": "The specific cuneiform sign is an amalgam of the signs for stick and flesh" (Kramer 1963: 237).

3. The various pain-inflicting tools and the quoted sentence are from Lancy (2015, p. 330).

4. Grove (2013, p. 87).

5. Peng & Nisbett (1999, pp. 741–754). I highly recommend the eye-opening and fascinating book by Richard E. Nisbett (2003), *The Geography of Thought: How Asians and Westerners Think Differently . . . and Why*.

6. Rawson (1996, p. 127); quoted in Lancy (2015, p. 332).

7. The full story of how gentler views about raising and teaching children came to prevail among many people in the West is one of the main threads traced in Grove (2013). See chapter 5, "New Views of Childhood and Children"; chapter 6, "New Views of Authority in Societies and Schools"; and chapter 7, "New Ideals for Human Life and Learning."

8. These facts are a condensation of the historical account traced in Grove (2013); see especially chapter 11, "Evolving Notions of Child-Rearing in Pre–Civil War America."

9. In ancient China, leadership was the responsibility of the group's oldest member, male or female [KJ & AP].

10. Evidence suggests that Chinese villagers respected the hierarchy and were disposed to comply with its directives. But the relationship is better characterized as one of reciprocity: the villagers remained loyal and compliant so long as their leader was competent and cared for them. In Japan and Korea, reciprocity was less central; the individual at the top of the hierarchy—due to age, title, and/or educational attainment—was accorded respect and obedience regardless of his competence or care [KJ & AP].

11. Consider the meaning of the Chinese word for individualism: "Gèrénzhŭyì is literally translated as 'one person doctrine' but is commonly used to mean both 'individualism' and 'selfishness.' In traditional Chinese culture, an individual's talents were not allowed to develop freely. A young Chinese grew up expecting to serve his or her father and the emperor. To those who showed more than a slight tendency to follow their own predilections, social sanctions brought swift and inevitable punishment. During the Cultural Revolution . . . , gèrénzhŭyì became an all-purpose pejorative (much as communist was in the United States during the McCarthy era)." Hu, Grove, & Enping (2010, p. 55).

12. *Analects* 7:1. The Chinese characters on which this saying is based—*shùérbúzùo*—have been variously translated by different authorities. Among half a dozen options are "I transmit rather than innovate. I trust in and love the ancient ways" (Slingerlands); and "A transmitter and not a maker, believing in and loving the ancients" (Legge) [KJ & AP].

13. From the *Analects* 15:24, translation of David Hinton. Dozens of quotations from the writings of Confucius and his disciples are easily found on the web. Some of them might sound familiar to you.

14. *Analects* 2:11 [KJ & AP].

15. For a thorough history and assessment of the Imperial Examination System, see He Gan (2008). He Gan's article includes the following paragraph (2008, p. 126):

First, the Imperial Examination System carried the principle of open examination, fair competition, and selection according to excellence. Officials were selected no matter what one's family origin was, and no nomination from high officials was required. The selection was done according to the result of the examinations. Second, the Imperial Examination System as a means of education and official selection at the end of education was part of and could not be separated from education. It promoted the development of education and society. Third, in the later stages of the system, the standards of talent selection were mainly one's understanding of Confucian classics, not one's actual ability nor the exploration of unknown fields. In other words, it focused on how well one learnt not how well one could perform, innovate or discover. Fourth, the aim of this examination was to obtain power, fame, and wealth by serving the country, but it was actually serving the Emperor, because the principle of conduct for the nominees was to do according to the Emperor's will. Fifth, it had built a bureaucratic society in which the officers were important, and other people were not important. Those who passed the examinations immediately became members of the nobility and the ruling class.

CHAPTER 8

1. Ripley (2013, pp. 106–107) [annotated].
2. In the anthropological literature, high awareness of a potential negative evaluation of oneself or one's family by others in the community is discussed under the heading of "shame." See, for example, Fung (1999) [annotated]. I do not use the word "shame" in the text because I anticipated that some readers could be repelled by the idea that East Asian parents deliberately train their children to become conscious of shame.
3. My referring to the American approach as "facilitative" is derived from Chao (1995) [annotated]. Chao notes that the phrase "facilitative model" originated with Hess and Holloway (1984, pp. 179–222).
4. My referring to the East Asian approach as "supervisory" is my own doing; it's not derived from the research literature. I am not aware that any rubric has been suggested to parallel "facilitative." After considering several options, I decided that "supervisory" best fits the East Asian parenting approach.
5. The contrast between American parents' goal of "optimization" and East Asian parents' goal of "exceptionality" was derived from Lancy (2015, pp. 161–162) [annotated]. Lancy comments as follows:

> A[nother] goal in the U.S. is that the child should be popular with peers and "well liked by all," which accounts in part for the extraordinary investment parents are willing to make in the child's extracurricular activity and in his or her wardrobe and treasure of possessions. This creates a striking contrast with the East Asian model, where high academic achievement is the primary objective and the belief is that the child should willingly forego popularity for exceptionality.

6. Chao & Sue (1996) [annotated].
7. This observation was offered by Ruth K. Chao in her 1994 paper, "Beyond Parental Control and Authoritarian Parenting Style: Understanding Chinese Parenting through the Cultural Notion of Training."

8. LeVine & LeVine (2016, p. 118); italics added.

9. For readers familiar with Mandarin Chinese, note that the tone mark (third tone) identifies this *guǎn* as different from another *guān* (first tone). The latter, *guān*, is the one that is part of the often-used two-syllable word *guānxi* (relationship; *xi* is fifth tone, i.e., unaccented). *Guānxi* often signifies an emotion-laden human connection with reciprocal obligations [KJ & AP].

10. How Americans came to the belief that children are weak, fragile beings is one of the main threads traced in my 2013 book, *The Aptitude Myth* (Grove, 2013). See especially chapters 5, 6, 7, and 11.

11. Chao & Tseng (2002, p. 76) [annotated]. The quote is attributed to Stewart et al. (1998, pp. 345–358).

Later on page 76, Chao & Tseng (2002) review the work of other researchers who "found that both sons and daughters who perceived their mothers and fathers as more domineering also perceived them as less warm." "Family-based" control was positively correlated with warmth, whereas "domineering control" was negatively correlated with warmth. Among Chinese adolescents, control may be perceived very positively unless it includes aspects of harshness or hostility. Cited are Lau & Cheung (1987, pp. 726–729) and Lau et al. (1990, pp. 674–677).

12. Except as noted below, this section relies on White & LeVine (1986) [annotated], and on Merry White's book published in 1987, *The Japanese Educational Challenge: A Commitment to Children*, especially chapter 2, "Motivation and Mores: Cultural Prerequisites for Learning."

13. In the text, I do not discuss certain Japanese terms for parental supervision because I anticipated that some readers could be repelled by the rigorous expectations they place on the mother. The best-known term of this type is *kyōiku mama*, "education mother." Well known among researchers, it even was mentioned in a 1987 U.S. Department of Education publication. See Simons (1991) [annotated]. About *kyōiku mama*–style parenting, Simons writes:

> Behind every Japanese student who scores high on examinations . . . stands a mother who is supportive, aggressive, and completely involved in her child's education. She studies [so she can participate with him in learning], she packs lunches, she waits for hours in lines to register her child for exams, and waits again in the hallways for hours while he takes them. She denies herself TV so her child can study in quiet, and she stirs noodles at 11:00 P.M. for the scholar's snack. She shuttles her youngsters from exercise class to rhythm class to calligraphy class to piano lessons [to] swimming and martial arts instruction. Every day she helps with homework, hires tutors, and works part-time to pay for *juku* [after-school school, often called "cram school"]. Sometimes she enrolls in "mother's class" so she can help with drills at home. (1991, p. 59)

Another term that I elected to not discuss in the text is *wakaraseru*, which means "getting the child to understand." But it means something utterly different from giving the child an easy-to-grasp explanation. *Wakaraseru* is the process of engaging the child in the goals the mother has set. It is guided by the seemingly contradictory principle that the mother must never go against the child. White & LeVine (1986) write:

Where an American might view this manipulation of the child through indulgence as preventing the development of a strong self-will; the Japanese mother sees long-term benefits of self-motivated cooperation and real commitment from her strategy of keeping the child happy and engaged.

Taniuchi (1982) describes a process in which intimacy and supportive attention to a child are used by the mother to teach the child social standards and the need to work hard to achieve and be valued in society. Other investigators (Conroy et al., 1980) cite "Love-oriented" techniques, rather than "power-assertive" methods in disciplining children. (1986, p. 29)

14. The discussion of *shitsuke* relies on Hendry (1986) [annotated]. Hendry references *shitsuke* throughout her book, beginning on page 11.

I discovered that *shitsuke* also is well known in Japanese manufacturing circles, as part of the structured "5S" program to systematically achieve total organization, cleanliness, and standardization in the workplace. The five S's are *Seiri* (tidiness), *Seiton* (orderliness), *Seiso* (cleanliness), *Seiketsu* (standardization), and *Shitsuke* (discipline). "Once true shitsuke is achieved, personnel voluntarily observe cleanliness and orderliness at all times, without having to be reminded by management." Visit www.eesemi.com/5S.htm.

15. Hendry cites *Nihon Minzokugaku Jiten* (Japanese Folklore Dictionary), 1979.

16. Hendry (1986, p. 156); italics added.

17. White (1987) attributes "authentic in intent and cooperative in spirit" to Kumagai (1981). White's next paragraph reads in part as follows:

It is very hard to catch the nuances [of *sunao*] in English: naïveté, naturalness, simplicity, mildness, gentleness, and straightforwardness are part of the meaning. Kumagai, meanwhile, points out that the English translation "obedience" implies subordination and lack of self-determination, but asserts that sunao "assumes cooperation to be an act of affirmation of the self" (Kumagai, 1981, p. 261). (White, 1987)

18. As referenced by White (1986, p. 87), the well-known psychologist and author Takeo Doi wrote that *sunao* means guileless, straightforward, and amenable (Doi, 1973).

19. The response in Japanese is *Mō sukoshi gambaru hō ga ii to omoimasu*. See Singleton (1989) [annotated].

CHAPTER 9

1. Damrow (2014 [annotated].
2. Damrow (2014, pp. 100).
3. Chen & Uttal (1988, pp. 355–356) [annotated]. The families studied by Chen and Uttal were in Beijing and the Chicago area; the children were pupils in the first, third, and fifth grades.
4. This finding concerned an imagined mathematics test. Chen and Uttal report that "[v]ery similar results were found when the question was phrased in terms of a reading test" (1988, p. 356).

5. Chen & Uttal (1988, pp. 356). The researchers also discovered that the American mothers were far more likely to express satisfaction with their child's school performance if their child liked school. For the Chinese, the children's liking for school had far less effect on the mothers' satisfaction with their performance. This finding was highly significant ($p < .001$).

6. A cross-cultural factor could help explain findings such as these in which the responses from Americans lie toward the high and/or low ends of the scale. As discussed in the "Creativity" section of chapter 11, East Asians' thought patterns are "dialectical," which means that they seek a "middle way" between extreme options and avoid "right vs. wrong" judgments. Americans tend rather strongly to dichotomize. When people answer surveys with a range of choices, thinking styles affect their choices. Thinking that's dialectical leads to responses that cluster toward the middle; thinking that dichotomizes lead to responses nearer the margins. See Harzing (2006) and Hamamura et al. (2008). Thank you to my private editor, Kay M. Jones, for finding these journal articles for me.

7. See Stevenson & Stigler (1992, pp. 74–84) [annotated]; Stevenson and Lee (1990, p. 100) [annotated]; and Chao & Sue (1996, pp. 115–117) [annotated], in which the authors also cite earlier research findings. See also Chao and Tseng (2002, p. 83) [annotated].

Chao and Tseng note that Carol S. Huntsinger and Paul E. José, often in combination with other researchers, have carried out several relevant studies. In one, the objective was to assess whether the at-home academic training provided by Chinese American parents affected the social adjustment of their children. They found that the children's academic performance was positively affected, but that the children's social adjustment was not influenced (Huntsinger, José, & Larson, 1988).

8. Stevenson & Lee (1990) [annotated]. These findings are reported on page 76 and in figure 9 on page 77. In stating the percentages, I have relied much more on figure 9 than on the written words on page 76.

9. Stevenson & Lee (1990, p. 76; italics added). The quote unites sentences from two paragraphs. This finding was supported by the authors by referencing figure 10, which reported "mean z scores" that combined data about mothers' satisfaction with other data about each child's higher or lower scores in reading and mathematics.

10. Peggy J. Miller et al. (2002), [annotated], quotes from p. 234 and p. 232, respectively. Another researcher who compared American and Chinese mothers found that the goal of "building my child's self-esteem" was mentioned by 64% of the Americans but merely 8% of the Chinese. Ruth K. Chao (1995, p. 336) [annotated].

11. Chua (2011, p. 3–4) [annotated]. The list has been shortened and edited.

12. Abboud & Kim (2006) [annotated].

13. Abboud & Kim (2006, p. 56 [excerpts]).

14. Huang (2014) [annotated]. See also Teresa Kuan (2015) [annotated].

15. Huang (2014, p. 47). I have shortened and edited Huang's list.

16. Huang (2014, p. 139). I have shortened this story slightly and lightly edited it. The incident occurred in the United States.

17. My private editor, Kay M. Jones, says that she has been told by Chinese American and Japanese American parents that one reason they avoid large, all-school

events is because they don't know how to mingle and do small talk like Americans. But a parent-teacher conference is acceptable because it's a sit-down one-on-one conversation with someone they know (and someone who plays a critical role in their child's academic progress).

18. Fogel et al. (1992, p. 46) [annotated]. Fogel and his colleagues found that, in a teaching task, American mothers emphasized *why*; Japanese mothers emphasized *how*. See also Hess et al. (1986, p. 154) [annotated]. Citing an unpublished 1982 paper by Giyoo Hatano, Hess and his colleagues write that, in Japan, mothers more often emphasize the procedural form of the task (i.e., knowing how to do it), whereas American mothers stress the child's conceptual grasp of the task (i.e., knowing about it). They add:

> It is as if American mothers must receive testimony from the child that the concept has been grasped. Conversely, Japanese mothers seem to accept the child's placement of the block as sufficient evidence that the procedures for sorting were understood or, perhaps, would be understood.
>
> [The] Japanese mothers first attempt to get the child to adopt the appropriate procedure in its correct form. They then expect the child to infer the correct principle, or concept, of the task by repeating the correct behavioral form. This style of teaching can be traced to traditional Japanese training methods combining cognitive and performance skills ("from form to mind"), that are used extensively for training in the classic arts such as noh, Kyogen, and flower arrangement. (1986, p. 154)

19. Messinger & Freedman (1992). "The Japanese sojourners had been living in the United States for 3 years or less; they spoke Japanese at home and planned to educate their children in Japan" (1992, p. 34). About this study, the researchers stated that "[t]he Japanese toddlers' cooperation with their mothers suggests that intensive, interdependent interaction was a regular part of their experience" (1992, p. 36). The Japanese mother-toddler pairs correctly fitted twice as many shapes as the American pairs.

20. Azuma (1994, pp. 279–280; italics added). The research study originally was described in Hiroshi Azuma et al. (1981), *The Influence of Attitude and Behavior upon the Child's Intellectual Development*. I was unable to acquire a copy of this original research report.

21. This ambitious study is "Study 2" discussed in Ng et al. (2007, pp. 1245–1252) [annotated]. Ng and her team employed complicated procedures, barely hinted at in the text of this Discovery Step. The findings of this study reviewed in the text are not necessarily the ones that most interested Ng and her team, who were mainly interested in understanding more about *gŭan* (introduced in Discovery Step 8).

22. Ng et al. (2007, p. 1249), short paragraph at the top of column 2. These data are not presented in a table.

23. And they wanted to learn to what extent the mothers spoke with their children using positive, negative, or neutral statements, of interest because American critics often claim that Chinese parents are more harsh than warm toward their children. Positive statements gave an openly positive evaluation of the child. Negative statements gave an openly negative evaluation. Neutral statements gave no evaluation at all of

the child; not surprisingly, a high proportion of the mothers' statements were neutral. The table below quantifies the mothers' statements following their children's success.

Following Her Child's Success, Mother's Positive and Negative Statements

Following her child's **success**	Chinese mothers	American mothers
Percentage of positive statements [e.g., "Sounds like you did pretty good."]	41%	76%
Percentage of negative statements [e.g., "Your logical reasoning is flawed."]	7%	2%
Percentage of neutral statements [e.g., "Did you understand the questions?"]	52%	22%

Following their children's success on a puzzle-solving task, average of the percentages of mothers' positive, negative, and neutral statements.

Based on data in Ng et al. (2007, p. 1249, table 3). The table above uses data from table 3 in Ng et al. (2007) but does not reproduce the table.

The table below quantifies the mothers' statements following their children's failures.

Following Her Child's Failure, Mother's Positive and Negative Statements

Following her child's **failure**	Chinese mothers	American mothers
Percentage of positive statements [e.g., "Sounds like you did pretty good."]	6%	25%
Percentage of negative statements [e.g., "Your logical reasoning is flawed."]	40%	17%
Percentage of neutral statements [e.g., "Did you understand the questions?"]	54%	58%

Following their children's failure on a puzzle-solving task, average of the percentages of mothers' positive, negative, and neutral statements.

Based on data in Ng et al. (2007, table 3, p. 1249). The table above uses data from table 3 in Ng et al. (2007) but does not reproduce the table.

24. From Ng et al. (2007, table 4, p. 1250).
25. From Ng et al. (2007, table 4, p. 1250).

CHAPTER 10

1. On July 30, 2016, an article by Javier C. Hernández appeared in the online *Times*, titled "Study Finds Chinese Students Excel in Critical Thinking. Until Col-

lege." The next day in the print edition, the article appeared as "Chinese Students Better in Thinking, Till College" (p. A9). I obtained more details from the study's lead researcher, Dr. Prashant Loyalka of Stanford University, to whom I am grateful for his cooperation.

2. For information about measuring critical thinking, visit the website of the Educational Testing Service at www.ets.org.

3. The data are from a pilot study involving 21 universities in China and Russia along with comparable data from the United States. In China, the freshmen were attending 11 universities including one "985" university (one of the top 36), four "211" universities, and six nonelite (tier 2) universities. In Russia, the freshmen were attending 10 universities including two national research universities (two of the top 29), three federal universities, and five nonelite (tier 2) universities. As for the United States, the entering freshmen were attending doctoral/research institutions in the United States but not universities among the elite of U.S. institutions (personal communication from Dr. Prashant Loyalka, the Stanford-based lead researcher).

4. "Significantly outperform" is a quote from slide 25, concerning levels of critical thinking, in a PowerPoint presentation about the pilot study made available to me by Dr. Prashant Loyalka. Freshmen in the United States, Russia, and China were administered the test in their native languages.

5. Ravitch (2014).

6. My 2013 book, *The Aptitude Myth*, ended with "Seven Assertions to Think With" (chapter 18, pp. 165–174). Those seven assertions, each discussed in approximately one page of text, are:

A. Accountability for learning rests more with the parents than with the teacher.
B. Accountability for learning rests more with the student than with the teacher.
C. A child's mental apparatus is vigorous, robust, resilient, curious, and absorbent.
D. A child's mental development involves intentional adaptation to its environment.
E. A child's competence grows more strongly and swiftly with authoritative guidance.
F. Learning attainment is determined far more by perseverance than by "givens."
G. Increasing mastery of skills and knowledge depends on skill focus and knowledge focus.

CHAPTER 11

1. Damrow (2014, p. 100) [annotated]. See the beginning of Discovery Step 9.

2. During the late 1980s and early 1990s, East Asian educational policy makers were becoming attracted to Western child-centered teaching approaches. In China, 1999 was the year in which the government announced a new state education policy, "Education for Quality," which included many Western-inspired elements. For a critical overview and analysis, see Lin (2010). In the annotated bibliography, see three reports of anthropological research: Way et al. (2013), Kuan (2015), and Jin & Cortazzi (2006).

3. East Asian educators are not as committed as American educators to the "mainstreaming" of students with disabilities. On the other hand, East Asian educators practice what we call "heterogeneous grouping." As noted in the text, East Asians have little interest in the inborn aptitudes of very young children, so they virtually never see any reason to group them on that basis. As the students get older, adults start grouping them on the basis of their actual performances, which East Asians view as outcomes of greater or lesser levels of persistent effort.

4. One issue about which anthropological findings are not consistent, at least in my reading, is the extent to which East Asian parents academically prepare their preschool children. Some sources report strong efforts in that direction; for example, see Parmar et al. (2008) [annotated]. Other sources, most notably those describing the Japanese, report a strong belief that preschool children should be "indulged," never taught; for example, see Lewis (1991) [annotated]. (Note: Japanese Ministry of Education guidelines forbid the preschools from teaching reading or math!)

Based on the 40 years of research reports on which I relied, my tentative conclusion is that East Asian immigrants in the United States were more likely to teach and drill their preschool-age children, while East Asians who were living in East Asia were more likely to indulge their preschoolers. Note, however, that from other sources I have encountered evidence of change in Japan, at least among well-educated middle-class parents there. For an eye-opening 1996 news report about cram schools for very young children, search the web for "In Japan, even toddlers feel the pressure to excel."

5. My original intention was that this book would address teaching and classroom practices together with the question of student receptivity. In the end, I decided to deal solely with student receptivity in order to keep the book sharply focused. However, I did not remove from the online annotated bibliography the citations about teacher preparation and collaboration, teaching approaches, and classroom practices. If you're interested in those topics, I recommend these:

- Becker, Jerry P., et al. (1999). Some findings of the US-Japan cross-cultural research on students' problem-solving behaviors. [mathematics]
- Cortazzi, Martin, & Lixian Jin (2001). Large classes in China: 'Good' teachers and interaction.
- Grove, Cornelius (1984). U.S. schooling through Chinese eyes.
- Holloway, Susan D. (1988). Concepts of ability and effort in Japan and the United States.
- Kawanaka, Takako et al. (1999). Studying mathematics classrooms in Germany, Japan, and the United States.
- Marton, Ference (2000). Some critical features of learning environments. [mathematics]
- Paine, Lynn Webster (1990). The teacher as virtuoso: A Chinese model for teaching.
- Pratt, Daniel D., et al. (1999). Chinese conceptions of "effective teaching" in Hong Kong: Towards culturally sensitive evaluation of teaching.
- Stevenson, Harold (1994). Moving away from stereotypes and preconceptions.

- Stigler, James, & Harold W. Stevenson (1991). How Asian teachers polish each lesson to perfection.
- Tsuchida, Ineko, & Catherine C. Lewis (1998). Responsibility and learning: Some preliminary hypotheses about Japanese elementary classrooms.

6. See, for example, Salzman (1986) [annotated]; and Sato & McLaughlin (1992) [annotated].

7. Tsuchida & Lewis (1998, excerpts from pp. 210–11) [annotated].

8. Pratt et al. (1999, excerpts from p. 251) [annotated].

9. Bernstein (2016, p. 32, continued from p. 28).

10. The historical rise of this belief is traced in my 2013 book, *The Aptitude Myth: How an Ancient Belief Came to Undermine Children's Learning Today* (Grove, 2013).

11. LeVine & LeVine (2016, pp. 98, 133, 140–143, 155, 169–174). The LeVines prominently cite the findings of Ochs & Izquierdo (2009).

12. Damrow (2014, p. 99) [annotated].

13. According to the tally available on Wikipedia, through 2015 Japan and China together claimed 36 Nobel Prize winners, while the United States claimed 356 (starting with Theodore Roosevelt in 1906). More than 25% of the American winners were born abroad.

14. Zhao (2012, page 10). Significantly, this book was copublished by the National Association of Elementary School Principals.

15. In fairness, the term "cultural intelligence" does appear in Zhao's index. He recognizes that, in today's global marketplace, cultural intelligence is important. I agree with his belief, and I endorse his recommendation that "[w]henever possible, schools should develop programs that can provide students with opportunities to experience being a foreigner" (2012, p. 229).

On the other hand, I contest Dr. Zhao's statement that "[w]here [students] are forced to study for cultural or family reasons, they may be doing the job of learning, but they do not necessarily enjoy [sic] and instead experience significant psychological damages" (2012, p. 172). At least with respect to East Asian students in East Asia, the reverse has been found! For example, in Discovery Step 8, "Revealing How Parents Think," see the last few paragraphs in the section titled "How the Chinese Talk about Parenting." See also Stevenson & Lee (1990) [annotated]. And by the way, efforts to reveal that mental derangement or drug addiction was the fate of the daughters of the original Tiger Mother, Amy Chua, have all come up empty-handed.

16. My business partner, Willa Zakin Hallowell, is an anthropologist. She reminds me that, although anthropologists do look at situations and wonder what's going on, their method necessarily involves a first step of devising a hypothesis to explain what's going on. (She says, "That's how you get a grant to fund your project!") A hypothesis rarely is an example of deductive thinking. Much more often, a hypothesis is a tentative conclusion based on one's own and others' prior observations. It's a tentative conclusion that, in the new study, will be further tested and refined by fresh observational evidence of what's going on.

17. For these contrasts, I relied largely on Morris & Leung (2010) [annotated]; Niu & Sternberg (2006) [annotated]; and Fryer and Fryer-Bolingbroke (2011) [annotated]. See also Lubart (1990).

18. Peng & Nisbett (1999). I highly recommend the eye-opening and fascinating book by Richard E. Nisbett, *The Geography of Thought: How Asians and Westerners Think Differently . . . and Why* (2003).

19. Unlike the STEM subjects, performance in reading is difficult to assess and compare across cultures because of the wide variations in how spoken sounds are written. Think of the differences among how English, Russian, Arabic, and Chinese are written. How children learn to read varies widely as well. For an insightful discussion of Chinese students' learning characters, see Biggs (1996a) [annotated].

20. For a critical overview and analysis of China's "Education for Quality" policy, see Lin (2010). In the online annotated bibliography, see Way et al. (2013), Kuan (2015), and Jin & Cortazzi (2006).

21. See Woronov (2008, 401–422). The quotes from the Beijing art and music teachers are from p. 410.

POSTSCRIPT

1. Gopnik (2016, pp. 3–5).
2. Gopnik (2016, p. 10).
3. Gopnik (2016, pp. 21–22).
4. LeVine & LeVine (2016, p. 27).
5. LeVine & LeVine (2016, p. 21). The LeVines were colleagues of Bettelheim during several years at the University of Chicago. By the way, the LeVines view the famous pediatrician, Dr. Benjamin Spock, is giving worthy advice (2016, p. 13).
6. The notion that parents must do everything right or else their child's well-being and future will be seriously endangered was popularized during the second half of the 19th century by British philosopher Herbert Spencer, who was hugely influential in the United States. See my book *The Aptitude Myth* (Grove, 2013), chapters 9 and 10.
7. This conclusion is stated at the beginning and the end of Robert and Sarah LeVine's *Do Parents Matter?* (2016, pp. xxi, 191).
8. Many people presume that top students' adult lives will be exemplary, but in this book I say nothing about that. What I do say is that several researchers have found that the East Asian approach to child-rearing—or better, child-training—does not routinely drive children into mental illness. At least with respect to East Asian students in East Asia, the reverse has been found. In Discovery Step 8, see the final paragraphs in the section titled "How the Chinese Talk about Parenting." See also Stevenson & Shin-Ying Lee (1990) [annotated]. Stevenson & Lee acknowledge that Americans fear that Asian students "must experience great stress from studying so hard and that they lack vigor, creativity, and joy in learning." But, following their numerous extended observations of East Asian classrooms, they report simply that "[w]e found no grounds for these fears" (1990, p. 101).

9. Gopnik (2016, p. 191). She also observes that "parenting inevitably becomes focused on trying to ensure that your children succeed in school" (2016, p. 180). The thrust of her argument is that, just like American middle-class parents, American educators have been taken over by the "carpenter" mindset, which is not a mindset that Gopnik wants to support.

10. LeVine & LeVine (2016, p. 157; exclamation point in the original). The LeVines's views on Chinese parenting practices are virtually identical to mine. They even conclude their three-page discussion of how Chinese parenting promotes school performance by contrasting it with American parents' focus on well-roundedness:

> But they also strive to inculcate independence, autonomy, and initiative, regardless of schooling, which they consider separate from other aspects of the child's life and behavior. These American goals, in contrast with the Chinese emphasis on obedience and diligence, may not lead to better performance in school, which American parents see as only one of several arenas for achievement (sports being another). (2016, pp. 157–158)

Bibliography

Abboud, Soo Kim, & Jane Kim. (2006). *Top of the Class: How Asian Parents Raise High Achievers—and How You Can Too*. New York: Berkley Books. 209 pages.

Azuma, Hiroshi. (1994). Two models of cognitive socialization in Japan and the United States. In Patricia Greenfield & Rodney Cocking (Eds.), *Cross-Cultural Roots of Minority Child Development* (Classic ed., 2014) (pp. 279–280). New York: Routledge.

Azuma, Hiroshi, Keiko Kashiwagi, & Robert D. Hess (1981), *The Influence of Attitude and Behavior upon the Child's Intellectual Development.* Tokyo: University of Tokyo Press.

Bao, Xue-hua, & Shui-fong Lam. (2008). Who makes the choice? Rethinking the role of autonomy and relatedness in Chinese children's motivation. *Child Development, 79*(2), 269–283.

Becker, Jerry P., Toshio Sawada, & Yoshinori Shimizu. (1999). Some findings of the US-Japan cross-cultural research on students' problem-solving behaviors. In Gabriele Kaiser et al. (Eds.), *International Comparisons in Mathematics Education* (pp. 121–139). London: Falmer Press.

Bernstein, Marc F. (2016, August 24). Who should be responsible for student learning? Commentary section, *Education Week*, 28, 32.

Biggs, John B. (1996a). Learning, schooling, and socialization: A Chinese solution to a Western problem. In Sing Lau (Ed.), *Growing Up the Chinese Way: Chinese Child and Adolescent Development* (pp. 147–167). Hong Kong: Chinese University Press.

Biggs, John B. (1996b). Western misperceptions of the Confucian heritage learning culture. In David A. Watkins & John B. Biggs (Eds.), *The Chinese Learner: Cultural, Psychological, and Contextual Influences* (pp. 45–67). Hong Kong and Sydney: Comparative Education Research Centre [Hong Kong] and Australian Council for Educational Research [Sydney].

Biggs, John B. (2001). Teaching across cultures. In Farideh Salili et al. (Eds.), *Student Motivation: The Culture and Context of Learning* (pp. 293–308). Dordrecht: Kluwer Academic/Plenum.

Boe, Erling E., Henry May, & Robert F. Boruch. (2002). Student task persistence in the Third International Mathematics and Science Study: A major source of achievement differences at the national, classroom, and student levels. Center for Research and Evaluation of Social Policy, University of Pennsylvania. ERIC document ED478493. 34 pages.

Chao, Ruth K. (1994). Beyond parental control and authoritarian parenting style: Understanding Chinese parenting through the cultural notion of training. *Child Development, 65*, 1111–1120.

Chao, Ruth K. (1995). Chinese and European American cultural models of the self, reflected in mothers' childrearing beliefs. *Ethos, 31*(3), 328–354.

Chao, Ruth K. (2001). Extending research on the consequences of parenting style for Chinese Americans and European Americans. *Child Development, 72*(6), 1832–1843.

Chao, Ruth K., & Stanley Sue. (1996). Chinese parental influence on their children's school success: A paradox in the literature on parenting styles. In Sing Lau (Ed.), *Growing Up the Chinese Way: Chinese Child and Adolescent Development* (pp. 93–120). Hong Kong: Chinese University Press.

Chao, Ruth K., & Vivian Tseng. (2002). Parenting in Asia. In Marc H. Bornstein (Ed.), *Handbook of Parenting* (2nd ed.). Vol. 4, *Social Conditions and Applied Parenting* (pp. 59–93). Hillsdale, NJ: Erlbaum.

Che, Yi, Akiko Hayashi, & Joseph Tobin. (2007). Lessons from China and Japan for preschool practice in the United States. *Educational Perspectives, 40*(1), 7–12.

Chen, Chuansheng, Shinying Lee, & Harold W. Stevenson. (1996). Academic achievement and motivation of Chinese students: A cross-national perspective. In Sing Lau (Ed.), *Growing Up the Chinese Way: Chinese Child and Adolescent Development* (pp. 69–91). Hong Kong: Chinese University Press.

Chen, Chuansheng, & David H. Uttal. (1988). Cultural values, parents' beliefs, and children's achievement in the United States and China. *Human Development, 31*, 351–358.

Cheng, Kai-ming. (1998). Can education values be borrowed? Looking into cultural differences. *Peabody Journal of Education, 73*(2), 11–30.

Cheng, Rebecca Wing-yi, Tse-Mei Shu, Ning Zhou, & Shui-fong Lam (2016). Motivation of Chinese learners: An integration of etic and emic approaches. In Ronnel B. King & Alan B. I. Bernardo (Eds.), *The Psychology of Asian Learners: A Festschrift in Honor of David Watkins* (pp. 355–368). Singapore: Springer Singapore.

Chua, Amy (2011). *Battle Hymn of the Tiger Mother*. New York: Penguin.

Collier, J., Jr. (1988). Survival at Rough Rock: A historical overview of Rough Rock Demonstration School. *Anthropology & Education Quarterly, 19*, 253–269.

Conroy, Mary, Robert D. Hess, Hiroshi Azuma, & Keiko Kashiwagi. (1980). Maternal strategies for regulating children's behavior: Japanese and American families. *Journal of Cross-Cultural Psychology, 11*(?), 153–172.

Correa-Chávez, Maricela, & Barbara Rogoff. (2009). Children's attention to interactions directed to others: Guatemalan Mayan and European American patterns. *Developmental Psychology, 45*(3), 630–641.

Cortazzi, Martin, & Lixian Jin. (1996). Cultures of learning: Language classrooms in China. In Hywel Coleman (Ed.), *Society and the Language Classroom* (pp. 169–206). New York: Cambridge University Press.

Cortazzi, Martin, & Lixian Jin. (2001). Large classes in China: "Good" teachers and interaction. In David A. Watkins & John B. Biggs (Eds.), *Teaching the Chinese Learner: Psychological and Pedagogical Perspectives* (pp. 115–134). Hong Kong and Sydney: Comparative Education Research Centre [Hong Kong] and Australian Council for Educational Research [Sydney].

Damrow, Amy. (2014). Navigating the structures of elementary school in the United States and Japan: An ethnography of the particular. *Anthropology & Education Quarterly, 45*(1), 87–104.

Doi, Takeo. (1973). Omote and ura: Concepts derived from the Japanese two-fold structure of consciousness. *Journal of Nervous and Mental Diseases, 157*(4), 258–261.

Duckworth, Angela. (2016). *Grit: The Power of Passion and Perseverance*. New York: Scribner.

Eklund, Anders, Thomas E. Nichols, & Hans Knutsson. (2016). Cluster failure: Why fMRI inferences for spatial extent have indicated false-positives. *Proceedings of the National Academy of Sciences, 113*(28), 7900–7905.

Fogel, Alan, Marguerite Barratt Stevenson, & Daniel Messinger. (1992). A comparison of the parent-child relationship in Japan and the United States. In Jaipaul Roopnarine & D. Bruce Carter (Eds.), *Parent-Child Socialization in Diverse Cultures* (pp. 35–52). Norwood, NJ: Ablex.

Fong, Ricci W., & Man Tak Yuen. (2016). The role of self-efficacy and connectedness in the academic success of Chinese learners. In Ronnel B. King & Alan B. I. Bernardo (Eds.), *The Psychology of Asian Learners: A Festschrift in Honor of David Watkins* (pp. 355–368). Singapore: Springer Singapore.

Fryer, Marilyn, & Caroline Fryer-Bolingbroke. (2011). Cross-cultural differences in creativity. In *Encyclopedia of Creativity*. London: Elsevier, Inc.

Fu, Alyssa S., & Hazel Rose Markus. (2014). My mother and me: Why tiger mothers motivate Asian Americans but not European Americans. *Personality and Social Psychology Bulletin, 40*(6), 739–749.

Fung, Heidi. (1999). Becoming a moral child: The socialization of shame among young Chinese children. *Ethos, 27*(2), 180–209.

Gan, He. (2008). Chinese education tradition: The imperial examination system in feudal China. *Journal of Management and Social Sciences, 4*(2), 115–133.

Gardner, Howard. (1989). *To Open Minds: Chinese Clues to the Dilemma of Contemporary Education*. New York: Basic.

Gopnik, Alison. (2016). *The Gardener and the Carpenter: What the New Science of Child Development Tells Us about the Relationship between Parents and Children*. New York: Farrar, Straus & Giroux. 302 pages.

Gross-Loh, Christine. (2015). High pressure? What Asian learning looks like. In *Parenting without Borders: Surprising Lessons Parents around the World Can Teach Us* (pp. 167–191). New York: Penguin.

Grove, Cornelius. (1977). *Cross-cultural and other problems affecting the education of immigrant Portuguese students in a program of transitional bilingual education: A descriptive case study* (Ed.D. dissertation). Teachers College, Columbia University. University Microfilms #77-14,722.

Grove, Cornelius. (1984). U.S. schooling through Chinese eyes. *Phi Delta Kappan, 65*(7), 481–482.

Grove, Cornelius N. (2006). Understanding the two instructional style prototypes: Pathways to success in internationally diverse classrooms. In Siow-Heng Ong et al. (Eds.), *International Communication Competencies in Higher Education and Management* (pp. 165–202). Singapore: Marshall Cavendish Academic (Singapore).

Grove, Cornelius N. (2013). *The Aptitude Myth: How an Ancient Belief Came to Undermine Children's Learning Today*. Lanham, MD: Rowman & Littlefield. 189 pages.

Hamamura, Takeshi, Steven J. Heine, & Delroy L. Paulhus. (2008). Cultural differences in response styles: The role of dialectical thinking. *Personality and Individual Differences, 44*, 932–942.

Hamedani, MarYam G., Hazel Rose Markus, & Alyssa S. Fu. (2013). In the land of the free, interdependent action undermines motivation. *Psychological Science, 24*(2), 189–196.

Harzing, Anne-Wil. (2006). Response styles in cross-national surveys: A 26-country survey. *International Journal of Cross-Cultural Management, 6*(2), 243–266.

Heine, Steven J., Shinobu Kitayama, Darrin R. Lehman, Toshitake Takata, Eugene Ide, Cecilia Leung, & Hisaya Matsumoto. (2001). Divergent consequences of success and failure in Japan and North America: An investigation of self-improving motivations and malleable selves. *Journal of Personality and Social Psychology, 81*(4), 599–615.

Helmke, Andreas, & Thi Anh Tuyet Vo. (1999). Do Asian and Western students learn in a different way? An empirical study on motivation, study time, and learning strategies of German and Vietnamese university students. *Asia Pacific Journal of Education, 19*(2), 30–44.

Hendry, Joy. (1986). *Becoming Japanese: The World of the Pre-School Child*. Honolulu: University of Hawaii Press. 194 pages.

Henrich, Joseph, Steven J. Heine, & Ara Norenzayan. (2010). The weirdest people in the world? *Behavioural and Brain Sciences, 33*, 61–81.

Hernández, Javier C. (2016, July 30). Study finds Chinese students excel in critical thinking. Until college. *The New York Times*. Retrieved from https://www.nytimes.com/2016/07/31/world/asia/china-college-education-quality.html

Hess, Robert D., & Hiroshi Azuma. (1991). Cultural support for schooling: Contrasts between Japan and the United States. *Educational Researcher, 20*(9), 2–8, 12.

Hess, Robert D., Hiroshi Azuma, Keiko Kashiwagi, W. Patrick Dickson, Shigefumi Nagano, Susan Holloway, Kazuo Miyake, Gary Price, Giyoo Hatano, & Teresa McDevitt. (1986). Family influences on school readiness and achievement in Japan and the United States: An overview of a longitudinal study. In Harold Stevenson et al. (Eds.), *Child Development and Education in Japan* (pp. 147–166). New York: Freeman.

Hess, Robert D., & Susan D. Holloway. (1984). Family and school as educational institutions. In R. D. Parke (Ed.), *Review of Child Development Research* (Vol. 7, pp. 179–222). Chicago: University of Chicago Press.

Ho, Irene T. (2001). Are Chinese teachers authoritarian? In David A. Watkins & John B. Biggs (Eds.), *Teaching the Chinese Learner: Psychological and Pedagogical Perspectives* (pp. 99–114). Hong Kong and Sydney: Comparative Education Research Centre [Hong Kong] and Australian Council for Educational Research [Sydney].

Holloway, Susan D. (1988). Concepts of ability and effort in Japan and the United States. *Review of Educational Research, 58*(3), 327–345.

Hsin, Amy, & Yu Xie (2014). Explaining Asian Americans' academic advantage over whites. *Proceedings of the National Academy of Sciences, 111*(23), 8416–8421.

Hsu, Francis L. K. (1981). *Americans & Chinese: Passage to Differences* (3rd ed.). Honolulu: University of Hawaii Press. 534 pages.

Hu, Guangwei. (2002). Potential cultural resistance to pedagogical imports: The case of communicative language teaching in China. *Language, Culture and Curriculum, 15*(2), 93–105.

Hu, Wenzhong, and Cornelius Grove. (1999). *Encountering the Chinese: A Guide for Americans* (1st ed.). Boston: Intercultural Press.

Hu, Wenzhong, Cornelius Grove, & Zhuang Enping. (2010). *Encountering the Chinese: A Modern Country, an Ancient Culture* (3rd ed.). Boston: Nicholas Brealey/ Hachette UK.

Huang, Quanyu. (2014). *The Hybrid Tiger: Secrets of the Extraordinary Success of Asian-American Kids*. Amherst, NY: Prometheus Books. 264 pages.

Huntsinger, Carol, Paul José, & Shari Larson. (1988). Do parent practices to encourage academic competence influence the social adjustment of young European American and Chinese American children? *Developmental Psychology, 34*(4), 747–756.

Immordino-Yang, Mary Helen. (2016). *Emotions, Learning, and the Brain: Exploring the Educational Implications of Affective Neuroscience*. New York: Norton. 206 pages.

Iyengar, Sheena, & Mark Lepper. (1999). Rethinking the value of choice: A cultural perspective on intrinsic motivation. *Journal of Personality and Social Psychology, 76*(3), 349–366.

Jin, Lixian, & Martin Cortazzi. (2006). Changing practices in Chinese cultures of learning. *Language, Culture and Curriculum, 19*(1), 5–20.

Junger, Sebastian. (2016). *Tribe: On Homecoming and Belonging*. New York: Twelve.

Kao, Grace. (1995). Asian Americans as model minorities? A look at their academic performance. *American Journal of Education, 103*(2), 121–159.

Kawanaka, Takako, James W. Stigler, & James Hiebert. (1999). Studying mathematics classrooms in Germany, Japan, and the United States: Lessons from the TIMSS Videotape Study. In Gabriele Kaiser et al. (Eds.), *International Comparisons in Mathematics Education* (pp. 86–103). London: Falmer Press.

Keller, Heidi. (2003). Socialization for competence: Cultural models of infancy. *Human Development, 46*, 288–311.

Kember, David. (2016). Understanding and teaching the Chinese learner: Resolving the paradox of the Chinese learner. In Ronnel B. King & Alan B. I. Bernardo (Eds.), *The Psychology of Asian Learners: A Festschrift in Honor of David Watkins* (pp. 173–187). Singapore: Springer Singapore.

Kim, Uichol, & Soo-Hyang Choi. (1994). Individualism, collectivism, and child development: A Korean perspective. In Patricia M. Greenfield & Rodney R. Cocking (Eds.), *Cross-Cultural Roots of Minority Child Development* (Classic ed., 2014) (pp. 227–258). New York: Routledge.

Kramer, Samuel N. (1963). *The Sumerians: Their History, Culture, and Character*. Chicago: University of Chicago Press.

Kuan, Teresa. (2015). *Love's Uncertainty: The Politics and Ethics of Child Rearing in Contemporary China*. Oakland: University of California Press. 255 pages.

Kumagai, Hisa. (1981). A dissection of intimacy: A study of "bipolar posturing" in Japanese social interaction—amaeru and amayakasu, indulgence and deference. *Culture, Medicine, and Psychiatry, 5*, 249–272.

Lancy, David F. (2015). *The Anthropology of Childhood* (2nd ed.). Cambridge: Cambridge University Press. 533 pages.

Lau, Sing, & Ping Chung Cheung. (1987), Relationships between Chinese adolescents' perception of parental control and organization, and their perception of parental warmth. *Developmental Psychology, 23*, 726–729.

Lau, Sing, William J. F. Lew, Kit-Tai Hau, Ping Chung Cheung, & Thomas J. Berndt. (1990). Relations among perceived parental control, warmth, indulgence, and family harmony of Chinese in mainland China. *Developmental Psychology, 26*, 674–677.

Lebra, Takie Sugiyama. (1994). Mother and child in Japanese socialization: A Japan-U.S. comparison. In Patricia M. Greenfield & Rodney R. Cocking (Eds.), *Cross-Cultural Roots of Minority Child Development* (Classic ed., 2014) (pp. 259–274). New York: Routledge.

Lee, Jennifer, & Min Zhou. (2015). *The Asian American Achievement Paradox*. New York: Russell Sage Foundation. 246 pages.

Lee, Wing On. (1996). The cultural context for Chinese learners: Conceptions of learning in the Confucian tradition. In David A. Watkins & John B. Biggs (Eds.), *The Chinese Learner: Cultural, Psychological, and Contextual Influences* (pp. 25–42). Hong Kong and Sydney: Comparative Education Research Centre [Hong Kong] and Australian Council for Educational Research [Sydney].

LeVine, Robert A., & Sarah LeVine. (2016). *Do Parents Matter? Why Japanese Babies Sleep Soundly, Mexican Siblings Don't Fight, and American Parents Should Just Relax*. New York: PublicAffairs. 240 pages.

Lewis, Catherine. (1991). Nursery schools: The transition from home to school. In Barbara Finkelstein et al. (Eds.), *Transcending Stereotypes: Discovering Japanese Culture and Education* (pp. 81–95). Boston: Intercultural Press.

Lewis, Catherine C. (1995). *Educating Hearts and Minds: Reflections on Japanese Preschool and Elementary Education*. Cambridge: Cambridge University Press. 249 pages.

Li, Jin. (2003). U.S. and Chinese cultural beliefs about learning. *Journal of Educational Psychology, 95*(2), 258–267.

Li, Jin. (2004). Learning as a task or a virtue: U.S. and Chinese preschoolers explain learning. *Developmental Psychology, 40*(4), 595–605.

Li, Jin. (2012). *Cultural Foundations of Learning: East and West*. Cambridge: Cambridge University Press. 385 pages.

Lin, Delia (2010). The cultural dilemma of a knowledge society in China: The case of "Education for Quality." Regional Outlook Paper No. 24, Griffith Asia Institute.

Little, Todd D., Takahiro Miyashita, Mayumi Karasawa, Mari Mashima, Gabriele Oettingen, Hiroshi Azuma, & Paul B. Baltes. (2003). The links among action-control beliefs, intellective skill, and school performance in Japanese, U.S., and German school children. *International Journal of Behavioral Development, 27*(1), 41–48.

Lubart, Todd I. (1990). Creativity and cross-cultural variation. *International Journal of Psychology, 25*, 39–59.

Mangels, Jennifer A., Brady Butterfield, Justin Lamb, Catherine Good, & Carol S. Dweck. (2006). Why do beliefs about intelligence influence learning success? A social cognitive neuroscience model. *Social Cognitive and Affective Neuroscience, 1*(2), 75–86.

Markus, Hazel Rose, & Shinobu Kitayama. (1991). Culture and the self: Implications for cognition, emotion, and motivation. *Psychological Review, 98*(2), 224–53.

Marton, Ference. (2000). Some critical features of learning environments. Invited keynote address, Bank of Sweden Tercentenary Symposium on Cognition, Education, and Communication Technology. Stockholm, Sweden, March 30–April 1.

Marton, Ference, Gloria Dall'Alba, & Tse Lai Kun. (1996). Memorizing and understanding: The keys to the paradox? In David A. Watkins & John B. Biggs (Eds.), *The Chinese Learner: Cultural, Psychological, and Contextual Influences* (pp. 69–83). Hong Kong and Sydney: Comparative Education Research Centre [Hong Kong] and Australian Council for Educational Research [Sydney].

Medrich, Elliott A., & Jeanne A. Griffith. (1992, January). International mathematics and science assessment: What have we learned? National Center for Educational Statistics, Research and Development Report. Retrieved from NCES.ed.gov

Messinger, Daniel, & Daniel Freedman. (1992). Autonomy and interdependence in Japanese and American mother-toddler dyads. *Early Development and Parenting, 1*(1), 33–38.

Miller, Peggy J., Su-hua Wang, Todd Sandel, & Grace E. Cho. (2002). Self-esteem as folk theory: A comparison of European American and Taiwanese mothers' beliefs. *Parenting: Science and Practice, 2*(3), 209–239.

Mok, Ida Ah Chee. (2006). Shedding light on the East Asian learner paradox: Reconstructing student-centredness in a Shanghai classroom. *Asia Pacific Journal of Education, 26*(2), 131–142.

Morris, Michael W., & Kwok Leung. (2010). Editors' Forum. Creativity east and west: Perspectives and parallels. *Management and Organization Review, 6*(3), 313–327.

Murphy, David. (1987). Offshore education: A Hong Kong perspective. *Australian Universities Review, 30*(2), 43–44.

Murphy, Kate. (2016, August 28). Do you believe in God, or is that a software glitch? *Sunday Review, The New York Times*, pp. 4–5.

National Public Radio. (2005, November 4). Health for the masses: China's "Barefoot Doctors." Retrieved from http://www.npr.org/templates/story/story.php?storyId=4990242

Ng, Florrie Fei-Yin, Eva M. Pomerantz, & Shui-fong Lam. (2007). European American and Chinese parents' responses to children's success and failure: Implications for children's responses. *Developmental Psychology, 43*(5), 1239–1255.

Niu, Weihua, & Robert J. Sternberg. (2006). The philosophical roots of Western and Eastern conceptions of creativity. *Journal of Theoretical and Philosophical Psychology, 26*, 18–38.

Ochs, Elinor, & Carolina Izquierdo. (2009). Responsibility in childhood: Three developmental trajectories. *Ethos, 37*, 323–342.

Ouyang, Huhua. (2003). Resistance to the communicative method of language instruction within a progressive Chinese University. In Kathryn M. Anderson-Levitt (Ed.), *Local Meanings, Global Schooling: Anthropology and World Culture Theory* (pp. 122–140). New York: Palgrave Macmillan.

Paine, Lynn Webster. (1990). The teacher as virtuoso: A Chinese model for teaching. *Teachers College Record, 92*(1), 49–81.

Park, Young-Shin, & Uichol Kim. (2006). Family, parent-child relationship, and academic achievement in Korea: Indigenous cultural and psychological analysis. In Uichol Kim et al. (Eds.), *Indigenous and Cultural Psychology: Understanding People in Context* (pp. 421–443). New York: Springer.

Parmar, Parminder, Sara Harkness, & Charles M. Super. (2008). Teacher or playmate? Asian immigrant and Euro-American parents' participation in their young children's daily activities. *Social Behavior and Personality, 36*(2), 163–176.

Peak, Lois. (1991). Training learning skills and attitudes in Japanese early education settings. In Barbara Finkelstein et al. (Eds.), *Transcending Stereotypes: Discovering Japanese Culture and Education* (pp. 96–108). Boston: Intercultural Press.

Peng, Kaiping, & Richard E. Nisbett. (1999). Culture, dialectics, and reasoning about contradiction. *American Psychologist, 54*(9), 741–754.

Pomerantz, Eva M., Lili Qin, Qian Wang, & Huichang Chen. (2011). Changes in early adolescents' sense of responsibility to parents in the United States and China: Implications for academic functioning. *Child Development, 82*(4), 1136–1151. Also available at NIH Public Access.

Pratt, Daniel D. (1991). Conceptions of self within China and the United States: Contrasting foundations for adult education. *International Journal of Intercultural Relations, 15*(3), 285–310.

Pratt, Daniel D., Mavis Kelly, & Winnie S. S. Wong. (1999). Chinese conceptions of "effective teaching" in Hong Kong: Towards culturally sensitive evaluation of teaching. *International Journal of Lifelong Education, 18*(4), 241–258.

Ravitch, Diane. (2014, December 3). "What you need to know about the international test scores." *Huffington Post* blog. Retrieved from http://www.huffingtonpost.com/diane-ravitch/international-test-scores_b_4379533.html

Rawson, Beryl. (1996). *Marriage, divorce, and children in ancient Rome*. Oxford: Clarendon Press.

Ripley, Amanda. (2013). *The Smartest Kids in the World: And How They Got That Way*. New York: Simon & Schuster. 307 pages.

Sahlberg, Pasi. (2015). *Finnish Lessons 2.0*. New York: Teachers College Press.

Salili, Farideh. (1996). Accepting personal responsibility for learning. In David A. Watkins & John B. Biggs (Eds.), *The Chinese Learner: Cultural, Psychological, and Contextual Influences* (pp. 85–105). Hong Kong and Sydney: Comparative Education Research Centre [Hong Kong] and Australian Council for Educational Research [Sydney].

Salzman, Mark. (1986). *Iron & Silk*. New York: Knopf Doubleday. 224 pages.

Samuelowicz, K. (1987). Learning problems of overseas students: Two sides of a story. *Higher Education Research & Development, 6*, 121–134.

Sato, Nancy, & Milbrey W. McLaughlin. (1992). Context matters: Teaching in Japan and the United States. *Phi Delta Kappan, 73*(1), 359–366.

Schneider, Barbara, & Yongsook Lee. (1990). A model for academic success: The school and home environment of East Asian students. *Anthropology & Education Quarterly, 21*(4), 358–377.

Shimahara, Nobuo K., & Akira Sakai. (1995). *Learning to Teach in Two Cultures: Japan and the United States*. New York: Garland. 259 pages.

Simons, Carol. (1991). The education mother (*kyōiku mama*). In Barbara Finkelstein et al. (Eds.), *Transcending Stereotypes: Discovering Japanese Culture and Education* (pp. 58–65). Boston: Intercultural Press.

Singleton, John. (1989). *Gambaru*: A Japanese cultural theory of learning. In J. J. Shields (Ed.), *Japanese Schooling: Patterns of Socialization, Equality, and Political Control* (pp. 1–8). University Park: Pennsylvania State University Press.

Spence, Janet T. (1985). Achievement American style: The rewards and costs of individualism. *American Psychologist, 40*(12), 1285–1295.

Stafford, Charles. (1995). *The Roads of Chinese Childhood: Learning and Identification in Angang*. Cambridge: Cambridge University Press. 213 pages.

Stevenson, Harold. (1994). Moving away from stereotypes and preconceptions: Students and their education in East Asia and the United States. In Patricia M. Greenfield & Rodney R. Cocking (Eds.), *Cross-Cultural Roots of Minority Child Development* (Classic ed., 2014) (pp. 313–319). New York: Routledge.

Stevenson, Harold W., & Shin-Ying Lee. (1990). Contexts for achievement: A study of American, Chinese, and Japanese children. *Monographs of the Society for Research in Child Development, 55*(1–2), Serial No. 221. New York: Wiley. 119 pages.

Stevenson, Harold W., & James W. Stigler. (1992). *The Learning Gap: Why Our Schools Are Failing and What We Can Learn from Japanese and Chinese Education*. New York: Simon & Schuster (Touchstone). 237 pages.

Stewart, Sunita Mahtani, Nirmala Rao, Michael H. Bond, Catherine McBride-Chang, Richard Fielding, & Betsy D. Kennard. (1998). Chinese dimensions of parenting: Broadening Western predictors and outcomes. *International Journal of Psychology, 33*, 345–358.

Stigler, James, & Harold W. Stevenson. (1991). How Asian teachers polish each lesson to perfection. *American Educator, 15*(1), 12–21, 43–47.

Tang, Catherine. (1996). Collaborative learning: The latent dimension in Chinese students' learning. In David A. Watkins & John B. Biggs (Eds.), *The Chinese*

Learner: Cultural, Psychological, and Contextual Influences (pp. 183–204). Hong Kong and Sydney: Comparative Education Research Centre [Hong Kong] and Australian Council for Educational Research [Sydney].

Taniuchi, Lois. (1982). *The psychological transition from home to school and the development of Japanese children's attitudes toward learning* (Unpublished manuscript). Harvard Graduate School of Education, Cambridge, Massachusetts.

Tsuchida, Ineko, & Catherine C. Lewis. (1998). Responsibility and learning: Some preliminary hypotheses about Japanese elementary classrooms. In Thomas Rohlen & Gerald LeTendre (Eds.), *Teaching and Learning in Japan* (pp. 191–212). Cambridge: Cambridge University Press.

Tweed, Roger B., & Darrin R. Lehman. (2002). Learning considered within a cultural context: Confucian and Socratic approaches. *American Psychologist, 57*(2), 89–99.

van Egmond, Marieke C., Ulrich Kühnen, & Jin Li. (2013). Mind and virtue: The meaning of learning, a matter of culture. *Learning, Culture, and Social Organization, 2*(3), 208–216.

Wang, Qi, & Michelle D. Leichtman. (2000). Same beginnings, different stories: A comparison of American and Chinese Children's narratives. *Child Development, 71*(5), 1329–1346.

Watkins, David. (2000). Learning and teaching: A cross-cultural perspective. *School Leadership & Management, 20*(2), 161–173.

Way, Niobe, Sumie Okazaki, Jing Zhao, Xinyin Chen, Hirokazu Yoshikawa, Yueming Jia, & Huihua Deng. (2013). Social and emotional parenting: Mothering in a changing Chinese society. *Asian American Journal of Psychology, 4*(1), 61–70.

White, Merry. (1987). *The Japanese Educational Challenge: A Commitment to Children*. New York: Touchstone. 224 pages.

White, Merry I., & Robert A. LeVine. (1986). What is an *ii ko* (good child)? In Harold Stevenson et al. (Eds.), *Child Development and Education in Japan* (pp. 59–62). New York: Freeman.

Woronov, Terry E. (2008). Raising quality, fostering "creativity": Ideologies and practices of educational reform in Beijing. *Anthropology & Education Quarterly, 39*(4), 401–422.

Wu, David Y. H. (1996). Parental control: Psychocultural interpretations of Chinese patterns of socialization. In Sing Lau (Ed.), *Growing Up the Chinese Way: Chinese Child and Adolescent Development* (pp. 1–28). Hong Kong: Chinese University Press.

Wu, Peixia, Clyde C. Robinson, Chongming Yang, Craig H. Hart, Susanne F. Olsen, Christin L. Porter, Shenghua Jin, Jianzhong Wo, & Xinzi Wu. (2002). Similarities and differences in mothers' parenting of preschoolers in China and the United States. *International Journal of Behavioral Development, 26*(6), 481–491.

Zhao, Yong. (2012). *World Class Learners: Educating Creative and Entrepreneurial Students*. Newbury Park, CA: Sage. 288 pages.

Zhu, Ying, Li Zhang, Jin Fan, & Shihui Han. (2007). Neural basis of cultural influence on self-representation. *NeuroImage, 34*(3), 1310–1316.

A Note about the Online Annotated Bibliography
Online at TheDriveToLearn.info

It is very common for a nonfiction book to include, on its final pages, a bibliography of sources that were consulted by the author during preparation of the text. But for *The Drive to Learn*, that seemed inadequate. The reason is the humane, qualitative nature of its underlying research.

Familiarity with the anthropological research on which this book is based will aid your grasp of its message. Anthropological research has a here-and-now quality that many other types of research lack because it often involves an individual or small team entering a society to try to understand it *from an insider's perspective*. The researchers build relationships with local people and, in some cases, live among them for months as "participant-observers." Their research reports include not only their findings but also background details about the society, an overview of what prior researchers have learned, and descriptions of revealing events that illustrate their findings.

Therefore, available online is an *annotated* bibliography of the key sources for this book.

WHAT'S INCLUDED IN THE ONLINE ANNOTATED BIBLIOGRAPHY

When you visit TheDriveToLearn.info, you'll find a more detailed introduction, plus 100 entries. Each entry begins with a "citation"—the author, date, title, and containing volume of the research report. Immediately following is my "annotation"—my overview or summary of that report. The annotations are compact; the most extensive ones are only about 300 words long.

There is no expectation that you will read all 100 annotations. I've made them available so that you can consult one or more of them to attain a better understanding of what I say in the text.

THE HIGHLY RECOMMENDED ANNOTATIONS

It's possible that you'll find this whole topic so fascinating, or so applicable to your parenting or teaching, that you'd like to learn more about this field of inquiry. If that's the case, I have designated as "highly recommended" 15 of the annotations, each indicated by an asterisk (*) at the beginning of the annotation. Reading all 15 will give you a good overview of the nature of this type of research, and of many important findings. Here are the 15 recommended annotations. Note: "et al." [*et alia*] indicates that there are additional authors (more than two).

1. *Biggs, John (1996b). Western misperceptions of the Confucian heritage learning culture. [book chapter]
2. *Chao, Ruth K., & Vivian Tseng (2002). Parenting in Asia. [book chapter]
3. *Cortazzi, Martin, & Lixian Jin (1996). Cultures of learning: Language classrooms in China. [book chapter]
4. *Damrow, Amy (2014). Navigating the structures of elementary school in the United States and Japan: An ethnography of the particular. [journal article]
5. *Heine, Steven J., et al. (2001). Divergent consequences of success and failure in Japan and North America. [journal article]
6. *Hess, Robert D., & Hiroshi Azuma (1991). Cultural support for schooling: Contrasts between Japan and the United States. [journal article]
7. *Iyengar, Sheena, & Mark Lepper (1999). Rethinking the value of choice: A cultural perspective on intrinsic motivation. [journal article]
8. *Lebra, Takie Sugiyama (1994). Mother and child in Japanese socialization: A Japan-U.S. comparison. [book chapter]
9. *Lewis, Catherine C. (1995). *Educating Hearts and Minds: Reflections on Japanese Preschool and Elementary Education.* [book]
10. *Li, Jin (2003). U.S. and Chinese cultural beliefs about learning. [journal article]
11. *Miller, Peggy J., et al. (2002). Self-esteem as folk theory: A comparison of European American and Taiwanese mothers' beliefs. [journal article]
12. *Ng, Florrie Fei-Yin, et al. (2007). European American and Chinese parents' responses to children's success and failure. [journal article]

13. *Stevenson, Harold W., & Shin-Ying Lee (1990). Contexts for achievement: A study of American, Chinese, and Japanese children. [monograph]
14. *Stevenson, Harold W., & James W. Stigler (1992). *The Learning Gap: Why Our Schools Are Failing and What We Can Learn from Japanese and Chinese Education.* [book]
15. *Tweed, Roger B., & Darrin R. Lehman (2002). Learning considered within a cultural context: Confucian and Socratic approaches. [journal article]

I hope that, at least a couple of times while you're reading *The Drive to Learn*, you'll pause to visit the annotated bibliography at TheDriveToLearn. info in order to gain insight into "where I'm coming from."

THE STORY BEHIND THIS BOOK'S COVER PHOTO

One way that books acquire their cover photos is that someone combs through the myriad images maintained by the photo stock houses until a suitable one is found. In 2013, after tedious hours of online searching, I came upon the perfect stock photo to adorn my book, *The Aptitude Myth*.

Things turned out differently in the case of *The Drive to Learn*. I had no difficulty finding stock photos of "children doing homework with parents"; there are *hundreds!* But virtually all of them either portray parent and child having fun together while largely ignoring the homework, or imply that the parent has merely stopped by to briefly encourage or monitor the child.

After six hours of photo research, I had found only *two* acceptable stock photos, and both had disqualifying problems. So I hired a professional photographer, Takako Harkness, who in turn hired two Japanese-American models, and we convened a photo shoot. The outcome is the evocative photo that you see on this book's cover. Here are the features I needed it to evoke:

- The mother-child interaction is occurring *within their home.*
- The mother is *participating with* her child, not just encouraging her.
- The mother is actively serving as her child's *coach and trainer.*
- They might be enjoying this time together, but they're not just having fun.
- Their focus is a commercially available workbook, the type often bought by East Asian parents and assigned for their children to complete *in addition to* teacher-assigned homework.

These five features of this parent-child interaction go far in capturing the spirit and purpose of "Parenting with *Gǔan*: Seven Commitments to Your Child" that I recommend in chapter 10.